A Teacher Appears

An Introduction to the Ascended Masters
of the I AM America Teachings

Lori Adaile Toye

I AM AMERICA PUBLISHING & DISTRIBUTING
P.O. Box 2511, Payson, Arizona, 85547, USA. (480) 744-6188
www.iamamerica.com

I AM America Maps and Books have been marketed since 1989 by I AM America Seventh Ray Publishing and Distributing, through workshops, conferences, and numerous bookstores in the United States and internationally. If you are interested in obtaining information on available releases please write or call:
I AM America, P.O. Box 2511, Payson, Arizona, 85547, USA. (480) 744-6188, or visit:
www.iamamerica.com

Graphic Design and Typography by Lori Toye
Editing by Elaine Cardall and Betsy Robinson

Love, in service, breathes the breath for all!

Print On Demand Version

9 8 7 6 5 4 3 2 1

Cover Design by Lori Toye, cover illustration credits follow:

Flammarion, Camille. *Woodcut with Caption:"A Medieval Missionary Tells That He Has Found the Point Where Heaven and Earth Meet..."* L'Atmosphere: Météorologie Populaire (Paris, 1888), pp. 163. Digital image. N.p., 23 Jan. 2011. Web. 7 Oct. 2012.

Heikenwaelder, Hugo. *Universum.* Digital image. *Wikimedia Commons.* N.p., 4 Apr. 2006. Web. 7 Oct. 2012.

"During the 19th century, the Romantic conception of a European *Dark Age* gave much more prominence to the Flat Earth model than it ever possessed historically. The widely circulated woodcut of a man poking his head through the firmament of a flat Earth to view the mechanics of the spheres, executed in the style of the 16th century cannot be traced to an earlier source than Camille Flammarion's L'Atmosphere: Météorologie Populaire (Paris, 1888, p. 163) [1]. The woodcut illustrates the statement in the text that a medieval missionary claimed that 'he reached the horizon where the Earth and the heavens met,' an anecdote that may be traced back to Voltaire, but not to any known medieval source. In its original form, the woodcut included a decorative border that places it in the 19th century; in later publications, some claiming that the woodcut did, in fact, date to the 16th century, the border was removed. Flammarion, according to anecdotal evidence, had commissioned the woodcut himself. In any case, no source of the image earlier than Flammarion's book is known." (Quote from en:Flat Earth)

"*Journeys at youth are part of the education;
but at maturity, are part of the experience.*"

- Francis Bacon

Contents

CONTENTS

CONTENTS

Foreword

Dear Reader,

I have the privilege to invite you on a journey with the Ascended Masters, those beings who have lifted out of the illusions of time and space to enjoy the sublime freedom of integrating with the Source. It is said, when a student is ready, a teacher appears. In the case of the material you are about to read, the student who was ready was the author of this book, Lori Toye, and the teacher who appeared was Saint Germain . . . and then Sananda (Jesus), El Morya, Kuthumi, Kuan Yin, and several others. The innocence in Lori's early channeling is engaging, building for the reader both a trust in her process and an enthusiasm for her discoveries. Records of these beginning steps have been missing from her earlier books, tapes, articles, and personal appearances. Your timing in reading this material may be a reflection of your readiness to make the same journey Lori made. Seeking and accepting a Master Teacher establishes an indelible link with Unity Consciousness and the teacher Sananda counsels us that Oneness is now necessary for our survival. This book demystifies Creation and invites you into Oneness.

The information in *A Teacher Appears* came at the same time that Lori and her partner were guided to make the I AM America Map. This map shows sweeping Earth Changes; its information and vision came as a prophecy, sounding a warning in time for us to make different choices and perhaps realize a world that does not reflect the prophecy. A deeper understanding of these prophesied changes gives us the power to mend ourselves to avert cataclysms and to begin an adventure into a Golden Age. We are a necessary part of the healing of Earth, as we and Earth truly are ONE.

The meanings of the Earth Changes are elaborated in another book, *The Freedom Star* by Lori Toye. But briefly, some background behind the Earth Changes prophecy: The Earthly Mother requested a Divine Intervention when our misuses of her had reached dangerous proportions. The response came through archangels, Elohim, goddesses, gods, lords, Lady Masters, and Ascended Masters. These beings established fifty-one Golden City Vortices surrounding our planet. They committed their energies and Oneness of Mind to calibrate these Vortices to lift the planet, not only out of danger, but into an evolved state of cooperation and joy. To date, we have witnessed fire, wind, water, and earthquakes change the face of the planet, but we need to understand that these "elementals" are doing so in order to cleanse the mental and emotional bodies of humanity to bring us back into alignment and harmony. The brilliant inner light of Earth is moving to her outer shell, just as assuredly as our own brilliant light is coming out through us.

My journey to a Golden City Vortex began due to my discomfort living on the East Coast of the United States. I had long been carrying the I AM America Map and was becoming increasingly captivated by how much it looked like a treasure map with its five Golden City Vortices. The closest one to me was Malton (pronounced Mal-tone). I traveled to Indiana, where I felt an immediate shift in energy upon entering the eastern edge of the 270-mile-wide Malton Vortex. Camping there that first night, I saw people—out-of-body entities—moving en masse into the Vortex energy. I joined them and felt like I was swimming in a slow, spiraling wave that was cleansing and healing. The next day, I explored many areas within the Vortex and was exhilarated by the energies I felt. With successive trips, I moved closer and closer to the center of the Golden City Vortex, and finally I settled in Mattoon, Illinois, where I wrote an article for the newspaper about the planet's need to rebalance herself and my desire to form a group to assist this process. This gesture moved me into an email network of open-minded people, and from that network, we launched the group I had dreamed of. Our group does Ceremony; we study the I AM America material and work together for personal and global healing.

You will learn more about the Golden Cities and dynamic healing Rays used by the Ascended Masters, as you read, but here is the status of both: The first Golden City Vortex of Gobean in Arizona is well established. Through the work of the Ascended Master El Morya, the Blue Ray is emanating transformation by aligning the will to love. The work of the Ascended Master Saint Germain in Georgia, the Golden City Vortex of Wahanee, is charged with the Violet Ray, radiating freedom and justice for humanity. The Golden City Vortex of Malton carries the Ruby and Gold Ray and the gentle energy of the Ascended Master Kuthumi, better known to us as Saint Francis of Assisi. Sananda ministers to us with the Green Ray, bringing healing and abundance to humanity from the Golden City Vortex of Shalahah in Montana. And Serapis Bey is the Ascended Master in Klehma, centered in Colorado. He works with the White Ray of cooperation and leadership.

For further elaboration, you might want to look at another of Lori's book projects, the *New World Atlas Series*. It brings us twelve universal laws called Jurisdictions. These connect us to the cosmic truth of a harmonious and abundant life. The three-volume set shares three different sequences of evolution and Ascension (dimensional shift) within the fifty-one Golden City Vortices. In the first volume, the seventeen Vortices of the Americas evolve the capabilities of the I AM Race. In the second volume, the next seventeen Vortices in Asia and Australia evolve the ecological alchemy of our Oneness with the planet. The third volume explains that the seventeen Vortices in Europe and Africa evolve the inner marriage of the male and female aspects, birthing Unity Consciousness. The book you are reading now, *A Teacher Appears,* offers fifty-one lessons that form the foundation for this global way of thinking and being.

My connection to this material deepened when I felt compelled to travel, out-of-body, to all of the fifty-one Vortices surrounding the planet. It took many hours every morning for many months to become familiar with the contributions of these Vortices. Glimpses into these works of the Master Teachers were a constant source of inspiration, and throughout my marathon persistence, I was always treated like a Sister, a fellow traveler, and an equal. The Masters showed me wonders, worked energetically with my physical and finer bodies, and helped me to align my thoughts to the best and highest good. I learned that taking the hand of an elder Brother or Sister was a triumphant act of Unity.

If you want to explore this material further, Lori Toye's most recent books form the first half of the *Golden Cities Series*, continuing the liberation process for readers. *Points of Perception* deals with time compaction, cellular awakening, vibrational shifting, and why change is necessary. *Light of Awakening* chronicles our evolution, how the increase in light reaching us accelerates our awareness, how service creates freedom and transmuting our past lets us start anew. *Divine Destiny* shows how the Kundalini unifies energy fields, rejuvenates the body and self, and brings about harmony with others. The importance of desire is discussed, as is how to create the world you want to live in. An ancient map brings forward information which explains the origins of our disharmonies and why the use of the Violet Flame will bring us back into balance.

A Teacher Appears is the first book in a trilogy, followed by *Sisters of the Flame* and *Fields of Light*. These books set the new stage for New Times. The primary teacher is Saint Germain, who carries the history and future of the world with such a depth of caring that one's heart fills with appreciation. And appreciation is a turn-key for our time, for it is the opposite of fear, resistance and, atrophy. The teacher El Morya describes how appreciation sends out a loving energy which comes back to us, augmented with Divine Love, Wisdom, and Power. Kuthumi brings us the wisdom of non-judgment and our Oneness with the Earth. Kuan Yin gives a wonderful discourse on stilling the mind and emotions. And Sananda teaches us the art of getting along and loving one another.

The material in all of Lori's books is multi-layered and can be entered into from different levels. The techniques of mastery work their way into daily life easily and transform perceptions and therefore, possibilities. The Ascended Masters have created pathways that we can safely follow. They are very real and present for those of us who have, or who want to have, the eyes to see and the ears to hear. Saint Germain's clarion call is one that we can choose to hear or not. Our true Home and Love will always await us. *A Teacher Appears* invites us to a round table—a place of equality—in a most intriguing way: El Morya was King Arthur, Saint Germain was Merlin, and Kuthumi was Sir Percival. Where "two or more are gathered" is Sananda, Lord of this Transition, and the fifth Star is Serapis Bey, holding the Flame of Ascension to light our way out of the darkness. We are in good hands and this book makes these hands very reachable.

OM EANDRA
(a special blessing for the Earth Mother),
Elaine Cardall

Elaine Cardall is a study group leader in the Golden City of Malton. She is a vegan, mystic, teacher, healer, and writer of songs, prose, poetry, and plays. She lives off the grid, collecting Power from the sun, Love from the rain water, Wisdom from the wind and Oneness from the Earth.

Preface

Dear Reader,

My introduction to the Ascended Masters and their teachings was nothing short of memorable. I worked as a sales representative for a weekly newspaper and had an appointment with a potential client. When I walked in the door and up to the counter of the small health food store to introduce myself, the owner stood up, pointed her finger at me, and stated, "You have work to do for Master Saint Germain!" Intrigued, I asked, "Who is Saint Germain?" The owner motioned for me to follow her through rows of neatly tiered vitamins to her office. On the wall hung a picture with the words *Comte de Saint Germain* carefully scripted in gold letters on the painting.

As I viewed the antique portrait of the eighteenth-century Frenchman, I had absolutely no idea who he was or why I felt so drawn to his aristocratic features and the details of his story. I was twenty-two years old, and the owner of his framed picture further explained that he was her spiritual teacher, and also an Ascended Master. I had never heard the term, "Ascended Master," nor did I understand how Saint Germain, who had obviously lived over two hundred years ago, could be a contemporary. Afterall, it was 1978.

The economic downturn of the eighties forced a physical move back to my husband's family farm in Idaho. My next five years were filled with the study and the practice of Ascended Master teaching: meditation, prayer, principles of reincarnation and the immortal soul, and the use of decrees—the sacred power of sound. I absorbed the spiritual teachers' vivid biographies, which rewrote conventional history, and my perceptions morphed with their enchanting stories of love, courage, endurance, and compassion. In 1983 I was awakened in the middle of the night, and thought the prairie winds had blown in yet another thunderstorm. The room smelled of sharp oxygen. At the foot of my bed stood the Master Saint Germain; his aura crackled and effervesced with electrical Violet Light. Later that year, in a vision-like dream, four Master Teachers in white robes presented a map of America, its coastlines dramatically changed with new geography.

At that time I was able to connect with a few like-minded souls, a rarity in those times, and especially uncommon for a small, conservative farming community. We studied and discussed the *I AM Discourses, Life and Teachings of the Masters of the Far East*, practiced yoga, and shared vegetarian recipes. And while we were all a bit reticent about openly sharing our beliefs, we decided to take part in a worldwide healing. We gathered in a public room at noon Greenwich time, December 31, 1986, to recite together the healing words, "The ONE Light of Love, Peace and Understanding is moving. It flows across the face of the Earth, touching and illuminating every soul in the shadow of illusion." Literally millions of worldwide spiritual seekers also participated in prayer and meditation that day—a miracle, and don't forget these were the days before cheap phone rates and the Internet! This would later be known as the first *World Healing Day*. By 1987, Jose Arguelles' Harmonic Convergence—yet another worldwide meditation which correlated with the Mayan calendar and important astrological alignments—reiterated humanity's need to change, and the spiritual doors for metaphysical and spiritual new thought were flung open.

The funny thing about change is that, while our soul may achingly crave transformation, we often resist. This was my frame-of-mind in 1988. My marriage had ended. I had left acres of expansive farmland to view a steady stream of congested traffic from the front window of my two-bedroom home. I was no longer a farmwife and worked full-time with my youngest child in daycare. My two older children remained in private school and lived with their father. I saw them on weekends; a stark juxtaposition from my days as a stay-at-home mom. The thrill of newfound independence was quickly tempered with days of sorrow and regret. I attended a spiritual development class to deal with my stress, and the group facilitator asked each of us to share our individual insights from a group meditation. Everyone described the intuitive flurry of lights, or the expansive feeling of energy. When it was my turn, I explained that Saint Germain had appeared and clarified to me personally the importance of meditation. The facilitator looked a bit surprised. After a moment of silence it was Sherry, the local tarot-reader and co-owner of the spiritual center who stated, "Well, you must be a channel!" Others in the circle nodded, and while outwardly I appeared somewhat shy and detached, deep inside I knew this was the truth.

A close friend had attended the meeting and afterward questioned me about my meditations with Saint Germain and other Master Teachers. I told him that I had always thought this was a normal state for meditation, and in fact had spent the last several years perfecting this process of what I came to know as the "inner-dialogue." My friend was emphatic that I become acquainted with the phenomenon of channeling, and loaned me several books he had recently purchased on the subject. As our personal and spiritual relationship grew, I shared with him my experience of the appearance of Saint Germain and the dream of the Map with the four Masters.

My friend Daniel, or Dan as I know him, was a student of Edgar Cayce and familiar with the spiritual knowledge of Earth Changes. He, like so many of us at that time, was caught-up in the newfound excitement of a personal and global awakening and was particularly interested in experiencing a seasoned channeler. Together we visited a well-known local medium, a channel of the entity *White Water*—a Native American spirit-guide who gave counsel in private sessions. White Water claimed that he knew me well, and would be especially present in my life throughout the next year. He also told me that my spirit-guide *Mahani* was nearby, and to not hesitate to ask for spiritual guidance or assistance. I left the session a bit unsure of its reality, even though my own personal encounters with Spiritual Teachers in meditation mirrored a similar experience. I would later discover that channels or mediums work with different trance techniques, and relay varying depths of spiritual information and energy suited primarily for those asking questions, or for those present at the session. Dan was nothing less than exhilarated from the experience, and convinced that I could develop my skills as a channel. And he was especially interested in the information surrounding the Earth Changes Map.

I've described in previous publications how the *I AM America Map* was received, scribed, and printed. If you need more details, it's all there. Since the Master Teachers requested an emphasis upon the prophetic message of Earth Change, we placed our first publishing efforts on the *I AM America Map* (1989), *Freedom Star World Map* (1994), *Six-Map Scenario* (1997), and the *United States Golden City Map* (1998). Much of the Ascended Masters' teachings and prophecies are contained in the *New World Atlas Series*, the *Freedom Star Book*, and the *Golden City Series*. The book that you are now holding, however, is the full genesis of this wonderful material. Here is where you will find how anyone with enough inspiration, appreciation, and love can open to the dimension of the I AM Presence—the individualized presence of God. The original transcripts of this book, and parts of the *New World Atlas*, were received via voice clairaudient channeling and monitored by Dan.

There are several important points to help you understand this process. First, in my early days of channeling, I would repeat what I heard in a meditative state. It went somewhat like this: "He (Saint Germain) is saying . . . " and then I would repeat Saint Germain's words to the monitor. The monitor for the channeled session—in this case Dan—would ask yet another question, and the progression of the lesson continued. No doubt, this was tedious. In the pages that follow you will learn how I evolved my channeling efforts with the use of different visualization techniques. And with certainty, the continuous help, assistance, trust, and unconditional love that constantly streamed to me from my spiritual mentors contributed to my integration process.

Channels are just that: they provide a channel or conduit of spiritual energy and information, and direct the flow of that energy and information. In order to reach a level of consciousness beyond the veil, they must generate a physical and spiritual energy or expansion to meet the energy of the Spiritual Teacher. The Spiritual Masters refer to this process as, "energy for energy." For the novice, this energy is often generated from within, and inevitably the person engaging in numerous channeled sessions can suffer emotional and physical difficulties—burn-out. The seasoned channel will utilize the physical and spiritual energy of those attending the reading, and in fact, in the same way that some channels are more developed than others, some *sitters*—the technical term ascribed to the medium and sitter interaction—generate more energy. I became aware of this nuance during my second year of training, and spent time with an experienced "generator." She would sit in our sessions, and literally feed streams of healing energy to me until it permeated the room. This process allowed me to channel numerous times in one day without any fatigue whatsoever. It is also important to understand the role of the monitor, or questioner, in channeled sessions. Next to the Spiritual Teacher, they are extremely significant as they ask essential questions. Their conscious effort shapes and molds the material, and this passionate query adds dimension and depth to each lesson. All of my channeled sessions are recorded and then transcribed.

As I said before, this series of lessons originally accompanied the Earth Changes transcripts, from which the *I AM America Map* was created, and the first book in the *New World Atlas Series*. The original tapes were first transcribed into a 400-page manuscript on an old IBM computer, and then saved to a floppy disk. It took me over a year to find a compatible system to open the file, and then we printed the information out on pin-fed computer paper. From there, we scanned the document page-by-page and edited what we thought would best fit the Atlas series. The remaining lessons sat for years in a blue vinyl source file.

We referred to the file as the *Blue Book*, and would turn to it, especially when we had research questions. Dan and I parted decades ago, and just like hearing an old song or detecting a familiar scent, the *Blue Book* words take me back to the sweet lessons of innocent spiritual pursuit. In 2007 I shared the *Blue Book* with my editor for *Points of Perception*. She carefully perused its pages and read a few of the lessons. "Yes," she said, "this book needs to be published." She thought it was a vital foundation to all of the I AM America teachings. In the meantime, I finished two more books in the Golden Cities series.

When Elaine Cardall contacted our office in need of books and maps for her study-group, we were surprised. While similar groups had been formed in the past, it was rare for one to be formed in a small town in Illinois. Through emails and phone calls, we developed a friendship and helped to mentor her group's studies of the I AM America material. When I approached Elaine to edit *A Teacher Appears*, I wasn't sure if she would have the time. During her editing process, Elaine sent emails with comments like, "Today I was telling a realtor about the right and left hand technique for manifesting," or, "I am feeling a little urgency with this material, as if there is a window of right timing beckoning," and "I am lit up! It is the equinox and Sananda has ended this manuscript with, 'For as we gather you under our wings, we will continue to bless you and treat you as one of the flock that you are.'" In other words, as the Master Teachers often say, "There are no mistakes, ever, ever, ever." And thank-you, Elaine, for your help in shaping the words, pages, and structure of this cherished work.

This book contains small, but simple, lessons. Yes, isn't that how it usually starts? Interestingly, there are fifty-one lessons altogether—just like the fifty-one Golden City Vortices that light the prophecies of the Freedom Star. You'll notice as the lessons move along they get longer. As I developed my ability to transmit information, I could hold the channel longer. Also, you'll notice a lot of technical information contained in the lessons. Remember when I said that channeled guidance will be custom-fit for those who are present? Apparently Dan had, in Saint Germain's estimation, a unique background—in this case, past lives—in the sciences. Many of the Master Teacher's visualizations and spiritual ideas are couched in technical terms designed to uniquely inspire and incite his student's spiritual growth. We considered editing much of it, but couldn't. Cleverly hidden in the jargon were many pearls of advice much too precious to discard. Last, but far from least, this book is the story of a spiritual quest. Two young friends embark together on the ethereal trail with hopes of spiritual transcendence and the earnest goal of Godly self-actualization. Yet, in our sincere pursuit we are faced with the all-too-human challenges of loss, judgment, betrayal, fear, and limitation. So inevitably, this book is about the journey of the heart, and its never-ending tests of acceptance and surrender. I think the late self-development guru Stephen Covey illustrates this best when he paraphrased the philosopher Pierre de Chardin, "We are not human beings on a spiritual journey. We are spiritual beings on a human journey."

In the Light of God that Never Fails,
Lori Toye

This lesson addresses aspects of communication and the difference between a Spirit Guide, our Higher Self, and an Ascended Master.

Inspiration, Intuition, and the Higher Self

I'd begun experimenting with trance-work just six weeks before this material came. We had recorded twenty sessions, using a small-hand held tape recorder; as I entered into a meditative state, Dan asked questions. Some of the sessions had flowed very well and some did not. I often floated in silence, experiencing levels of energy and brilliant light which no human words can explain, so I did not try to articulate them. I'd worried about the lapses on the tape and Dan's nudging me, "Are you there?"

At this point, I'm curious if there is a better way to channel, and wonder why some sessions have such clarity and flow while others do not. The session opens with a blast of gratitude and such loving appreciation from the three Spiritual Teachers that my heart chakra burns!

⤳

Saint Germain, White Water, and Mahani are opening up the portal of communication through thanks and appreciation. It's interesting because from each one of their Heart Chakras is a beam that's projecting out and it goes right to my own I AM Presence. Saint Germain steps forward.

Connecting from our Heart Chakras through your I AM Presence is the most important aspect of our communication and we can communicate with anyone this way. Do you wish to ask questions of White Water or Mahani?

Question: "What aspect of myself do I need to develop to be able to communicate?"

White Water identifies with the lower level of the Spirit nature, where inspiration relates to more earthly things. You can communicate with him at any time and he will help you. The next level is intuitive, with a person or entity which is more like a guide who has been with you over many embodiments and is here only to help.

Your own intuition comes from your Higher Self; yet this other person is there at the same time. Do you understand that?

Question: "Yes, but there's no way I can differentiate between the two, right?"

They're very separate, very separate beings.

Question: "But when I intuitively have an inspiration, how do I know if it's coming from inside me or from my guide?"

If you direct a question toward this entity, or any entity, and you get an answer from that entity, then it's coming from them. When it comes to you, yourself, it is yours. The next level is the ascended level, where your Higher Self functions all the time. Do you see that?

Question: "If the Higher Self is functioning from the ascended level and aware of all levels at all times, why isn't it more forceful and interacting more to help us? Why do we need the help of other entities?"

That's the whole point of what this is about. It is necessary to take on an identity with the Higher Self to integrate. Holding this identity as you talk to these entities, you will better know who you are and become aware that you could also be the combination of the help of all the collective energy. Who you are would be associated with all the people you've known in your lifetime or in any other lifetime.

The past catapults you into the present and the present, into the future. While in the physical, it is necessary to raise your consciousness, always feeling your individualized part as your new and true identity. Feeling the identity of your Higher Self first, then with the three, White Water, Mahani, and Saint Germain, a fourth is born. Feel the fourth and always know that the fourth is the highest. Do you understand?

Response: "Yes, I think I do."

2

*How to manifest healing energy, opportunity,
prosperity, even money!*

Manifestation and Spiritual Development

If we're going to print the Map and even explore some of the projects and products the Spiritual Teachers describe, we need money. I work full-time as a graphic designer, and I'm a single mother. Plus work has been slow at Dan's agency. This session came out of our very tangible needs.

Saint Germain shows me with his hands, the same Vortex of energy that he had directed from his Heart Chakras to my Higher Self. He is showing how you can take the same energy through the center of the hand and direct it for healing or protection. You can direct it for whatever need you have, even for prosperity.

You can take the energy flow right out of the center of the hand and direct it toward the map if you need money to print it. Direct it with the right hand only. Push it out and visualize prosperity, money, opulence, and all that you need. When you do this, take the left hand and cover your heart, asking for the Divine Highest Good. Do this the same way for healing or anything else you need. Do you understand?

Response: "Yes."

See yourself as the Vortex and know that you are the Vortex within each level of your being. White Water uses the circle and stands within the circle, which is another way you can do this. Mahani does it through meditation, while my method is through precipitation. Whatever way you are more comfortable, you can do: transformation, meditation, or precipitation.

Response: "I can understand the relationship between meditation and precipitation but I am unclear about transformation."

Well, we have to change. We have to be willing to accept changes in order to precipitate that which we meditate upon. They are all interrelated and by practicing all three, you will find one that is more comfortable.

3

How can we detect Earth Changes?

Ancient Technology

This is a technology session. When I receive this type of information my head spins with numbers and formulas and I have absolutely no idea what they mean! Afterwards, Dan replays the tape and I wonder, "Whose voice is that?" To make matters worse, often I don't remember eighty percent of what was said. Amazingly, Dan drafts a sketch from this lesson and later we'll return to the Spiritual Teacher with questions and refine the drawing. This teaching introduces Mafu, also known as the *Master of Harmony*, and he shares an ancient device that predicts earthquakes and tidal waves—the *Archtometer*. Hmmm ...

Today we are greeted by all three, Saint Germain, White Water, and Mahani. Saint Germain usually says a different greeting but today just says "Greetings from the Great White Brotherhood," referring to the Brotherhood and Sisterhood of the white-light. There is another ascended being with him today. It's Ma something, Mafu, I think, I can't see it. He looks very Oriental and is carrying a stick with two balls on either side of it that rotate. I'm trying to figure out what type of product it is or its symbology. He is spinning it and it looks like a gyroscope, reminding me of the Earth rotating, with its distribution of weight and how the axis could tilt.

Question: "What makes the first shift in the Earth's axis? Is it the impact of a meteorite or the melting of ice at the poles, shifting the water?"

The shifting of water and weight. It's real obvious when you see this device.

Question: "Is the weight then shifted to the equator?"

The equator is the band of equilibrium. It is an arbitrary line, of course, but that's where you have the equal distribution of weight.

Question: "What causes the imbalance then, I mean, how does the water shift?"

Excess water, water that we have never had before, is coming out of the ecosystem. Shifting lands at this point of equilibrium would cause a natural shift at the pole. The impact of a meteorite would start the shift in the lands and the dust blocking out the sun would melt the ice. This creates the start of the imbalance of water. If we wanted to, we could plot this in terms of the equator by looking at what is happening near the equator.

Question: "How can we plot that?"

You can use a device like this, with a measuring instrument screwed through its center. You take even the smallest section that you can of land, divide it in half and put the center, fulcrum point of the measuring device on the latitudes, running it parallel to the existing pole. Starting with one hundred percent water in each ball, you figure out roughly how much of the land has gone. It doesn't have to be exact, but for example, if sixty percent of the land to the west side is gone and twenty percent to the east side is gone, adjust the portion of liquid on both sides accordingly. Re-establish the equilibrium again by moving the measuring device at the center of the fulcrum or tilt it until you get the balance, the equilibrium established again.

Question: "Does this predict Earth Changes?"

This device was used many, many years in the Orient. They used it to predict earthquakes and tidal waves and their impact. This has not been used for three thousand years. It will come back into wide use again and be a device that people will be able to use during the Time of Change in their own areas when they become concerned about the many changes that are happening. They'll be able to measure it exactly.

This ascended being is leaving now. I can tell he is associated with the Laws of Harmony. Saint Germain steps forward.

This will give greater accuracy with the map, the magnetism, and pulls and can help show all the climatic changes more properly, more exactly.

4

A Technical Explanation of
Spirit-to-Human Communication

The Silver Cord

The next day in a lengthy session we refine our drawings and comprehension of the Archtometer with Master Mafu. However, the session opens with the presence of four Spiritual Teachers. This introduction explains our connection to the realm of Spirit, and how consciousness communicates with various Spirit Guides, Spiritual Teachers, and Ascended Masters. As I enter into the trance state, I see beams of light that connect me to Saint Germain, Mafu, and the Spirit Guides Mahani and White Water. The thickness of each cord varies. As I enter the trance state I experience another explosive wave of heart-opening gratitude that exudes from the Master Saint Germain.

Saint Germain is present with Mafu, Mahani, and White Water. Saint Germain makes a reference to a Portal of Appreciation and how important it is. It is a way to communicate, which does not hinder thought vibration. I can see that it is definitely a beam which connects us and through which we communicate. As it opens up, you can also travel through the beam. Divine Consciousness travels through it. The varying degrees of thickness of this cord determine the ease of communication.

Question: "What determines the thickness?"

Openness. We all are interconnected but desire determines the thickness of the cord.

Question: "Is this cord from the Heart Chakra?"

Yes.

5

*Clarification on how the shift
will manifest.*

Heaven on Earth

In a series of unpublished sessions, the Masters El Morya and Kuthumi assure that we will have enough money to publish the Map. Also they remind us, "This is a project we have been working on for a long time." To give us further encouragement, the previous four teachers divulge the location of a Spiritual Retreat deep in the Idaho forest. According to Saint Germain, Dan and I lived at this very spot many years ago in Ancient Atlantis. We worked as a brother and sister team of mental health technicians for the criminally insane, away from the major lands of Poseid. We used different forms of treatment which included telepathy, hands-on healing, and water and vapor therapies. Later in post-Atlantean history, the site was rediscovered and used by Native American tribes.

But here and now, it is January, so on our first expedition into the wilderness we bundle up and pack our cross-country skis and army shovel for exploration, as well as a thermos of hot cocoa. After an excruciating trek through three feet of snow, we think we find the spot. No doubt, I get the feeling that I've been here before. We dig in the snow and Dan finds a large unusual shell and I find a large mass of miniature red garnets, literally welded together through the pressure of time. Dan takes the shell to the University of Idaho only to discover it is indeed thousands of years old. And I'm certain the red garnets hold healing energies that I need and I place them carefully in my basket of crystals with my bathing salts. As tired as I feel, I am also exhilarated. I am fascinated with the healing site, and even more intrigued that I had lived there in another time, place, and circumstance.

The next weekend we excitedly return with snowmobiles, and in the acres of white-on-white and hundreds of snow-capped evergreens, we get disoriented. We're not lost, but we can't seem to locate the spiritual site. Dan is quiet and I sense an air of both patience and aggravation with the circumstance. I feel totally responsible . . . what have I gotten us into? To make matters worse, on the way home, our pickup skids on an icy bridge and the snowmobile trailer jack-knifes causing damage to the truck. It seems an eternity as the truck swerves back and forth across the bridge, bouncing left and right against the guardrails. At any moment we could plunge off the bridge into the creek bed fifty feet below. Dan protectively flings his arm across my swaying body. And as unexpectedly as our slide began, it ends. Our hearts pound and Dan pulls over, bringing the truck to a complete stop. Fortunately we were not injured and later, after Dan drops me off at my home, I rush inside to call a friend. She exclaims, "I sensed something like that was going to happen, thank God you're okay!" That night as I tuck my five-year-old into bed, I hold her tight and kiss her cheek. What if it had been worse? What were we doing out there, in the Idaho wilderness in January searching for an Ancient Atlantean Healing Site . . . are we nuts?

Dan phones the next day to tell me that he relistened to the tape. Apparently we turned right, instead of left.

For the next week our relationship is a bit tense. The damage to the pickup was worse than we thought and will cost him a couple thousand dollars that quite frankly, he doesn't have. Crap. It's my fault.

Before our journey into the frozen landscape of alleged spiritual sanction, White Water sent us both the energies of the raccoon and turkey to accompany our travels. Intelligence, curiosity, fearlessness, and the power of disguise are attributed to the raccoon. Yet right now the colorful bird of thanksgiving seems like slang for "stupid."

The next week, Dan and I present some of the Earth Changes information to our local metaphysical group. They all seem interested and supportive and eagerly await the printing of the Map.

After a full two-week break, my energy recalibrates and I start channeling again. No doubt, our adventure into the Idaho wilderness was in reality a test of our spiritual fortitude and an opportunity to heal and align our energy fields. This excerpt follows a previous session that taught an arduous calculation of possible pole-shift. Saint Germain corrects the calculation at least three times, and finally we understand the three prophetic shifts. What follows is the gist of the "shift" message.

Saint Germain is present. We had the first polar shift, which was not very large. The second will go to a land mass and the third goes to an existing location that is now in water. We are working with the map.

The Greenland coordinate has an element of accuracy but the final shift is a different kind of shift. It is lateral, not along the longitude. A lateral shift happens because the spinning is altered; the actual rotation of the Earth will be affected.

They seem to be plotting this in a spiral from the present location, going out and clockwise.

There are a lot of other factors to be considered and there will be a lot of other things happening, which are not necessary to understand at this time. The final shift is a more dramatic shift because it will open up the etheric and this difference takes a precise calculation. It has never happened before, that the etheric and the physical will both be accessible here on the Earth. This is the final shift.

6

Where are the Golden Cities, exactly?

Golden City Portals

As we progress into the knowledge of Earth Change, the Golden Cities—which are prophesied spiritual havens designed specifically for humanity's spiritual growth and evolution throughout the New Times are introduced. Apparently the north-south axis of each Golden City Vortex follows the degreed position of the Earth's North Pole. Since the magnetic pole will constantly drift, and the physical location of the North Pole will also change position three times, each Golden City's orientation is clearly in a state of constant flux. Saint Germain assures that their locations are accurate and introduces the foundation of their structure.

Who cares about the future when you're in debt right now and have bills to pay today? The Master Teacher assures that indeed everything *is* okay.

Question: "Right now, the axis of the Golden Cities Vortices is about four degrees to the left of the present North Pole. Using Greenland, wouldn't they then be to the right of it quite a bit more than that?"

The Golden Cities are of a finer substance and need finer calculations than anything dealt with previously. There are a set of laws yet to be discovered in mathematics called interdimensional mathematics. The cities themselves comprise a dimensional weight which anchors them. They are anchored in the physical, as they must be for access, but the apex locations serve as portals. Also, the polar shift will bring the change in the weather patterns and prevailing winds. Do you have any questions?

Response: "Not about this but about my difficulty manifesting the money I require."

You are doing a fine job. Have faith and love your work. You have a great strength of belief and will complete this. Today, I AM sending an extreme amount of radiance, an extreme Violet Light. I AM here at all times. When you are frustrated or confused, call upon the Mighty Source.

We are enveloped in the Violet Light.

7

How to face other people's fear of new information.

The Light of God Never Fails

I have now completed a minimum of forty sessions. Most of the information is facilitated by Saint Germain, but occasionally I receive trance information from my higher-self and insights from White Water or my Spirit Guide. Some sessions are focused on past-life information, either for Dan or for me. This teaching proves invaluable, and is often woven into the context of a lesson to emphasize an unused or forgotten quality or virtue. Sometimes Saint Germain teaches in symbols that simplifies otherwise confusing information. Here are a few:

Shell: A symbol of life's eternal change.
Crystal: Clarity of Consciousness
Eagle: A symbol of continuity and balance, and especially a symbol for the Golden City of Klehma, near Denver, Colorado.
Star: Represents the alchemical process of discovering the "spiritual substance" within oneself.
Five Stars: Five stars that form a pentagon stimulates the soul's memory of those who lived in the ancient land of America, (Ameru and Atlantis), and kindles the remembrance of their important role and tasks to complete for the New Times. America was once five islands now united as ONE.
Pyramid: Symbol of a Golden City

Dan continuously questions the Spiritual Teachers about dates; especially concerning the prophetic Time of Change and the possible Earth Changes. After all, if this is something we are facing, it would be good to know when—right? Surprisingly, that answer is, "No." Even though the Masters and Spirit Guides have been willing to give some general time frame, they are emphatic that dates are only "reference points." That is, a position in the landscape of an ever-present now where one can evaluate or weigh probability. By definition, a *reference point* is placed so we can initiate comparison between actual events, prophesied events, and the possibility of their timing. This is an important nuance.

So when a Spiritual Teacher gives a date in this material, it is not carved in stone. And that is a good thing! This gives us time to practice many of the spiritual techniques and disciplines to change ourselves and hopefully effectuate positive change in the world. No doubt, "A change of heart can change the world."

The metaphor, uncertainty, and general nebulousness of the information are not easy for everyone to accept.

Simplicity is important, simplicity and truth. Be aware at all times of those who may not want your truth or this truth to go out. Be constantly prepared and aware, then there will be no problem.

Response: "Yes, I'm trying to get prepared for that by talking to the small groups and getting their feedback."

The largest element is the fear element that needs to be overcome in people who are not aware of this way of thinking and this path. There are even people within your small group who have the fear element and you must never take it on. Remember, you are peaceful and harmonious beings, seeking the truth and the light, and the light of God never fails.

8

The Earth creates stillness to experience the ONE.

Weather Crystal

Saint Germain describes a large mountain of pure crystal prophesied to form in the Time of Change—the Weather Crystal. This enormous crystal has the ability to stop or alter our human perception of time, therefore quieting Nature's elements and affecting the weather. This stopping is similar to the Taoist philosophy of stillness. According to the ancient Chinese, this is possible when the cycle of the elements ceases and the elements (i.e., earth, water, fire, metal, and wood) return back to the ONE.

At the end of this lesson, Saint Germain prophesies, "America is a great focus of light for the Earth. They (Americans) are torch-bearers . . . but America will be one of the first to experience the changes . . . the first to overcome . . . and again hold the light." This almost infers that in the New Times all of the American nations will somehow expose their own darkness, and through that important passage, will evolve their understanding of the light. With all of the political and social darkness throughout the world today, this prophecy gives me hope.

It is apparent that overcoming our own individual darkness is just the beginning of the evolutionary journey. Earth is tied to our spiritual quest, and through the cultivation of stillness, the aspirant encounters the ONE and is prepared for Ascension.

Question: "What will the purpose of the weather crystal be in our region, to even out the storms and temperature?"

The purpose is to break through a portal, not only a weather portal, but a time portal. The weather and the Elementals are connected to the concept of time. How you look at them and view them is how you measure a concept that you do not understand.

Question: "And does this crystal stabilize these factors?"

It will be used to stabilize the Elemental Forces, so that man will have an opportunity to experience timelessness. Having all of the Elementals in balance and keeping them there for a directed period of time will give a sense of timelessness. This timelessness will give the balance and the harmony needed to seek within and to raise consciousness to the ascended level. It will be used to assist and help the direction of the masses. Many people do this already through meditation but there will still be those who will not be able to accept meditative forces and never will. They must be given the peace that they need. And not only for them, but this would be a great assistance to others as well who experience it in the higher dimension.

Question: "Does this crystal control where the new time zones will be?"

Yes, it could and it is something that will be adjusted periodically. Again, the portal is where you can break through the skies.

I am seeing now how it works, by taking a specific area and controlling the Elementals. At a given location, if we were to measure it, say at two o'clock, you could keep it at two o'clock through a controlled environment. It's an ecosystem that has been totally allowed to be, so that the higher nature comes through instead of the following through in a process which is typical of an ecosystem.

Question: "What would this look like?"

Water generally has motion. What causes the motion is the interaction of water with the earth element or the air element. Fire, what causes the fire? Well, fire has the interaction with the earth element. What causes wind? Interaction again with the earth element. Each Elemental will be allowed to exist in its purest form without the interaction. It's like a meditative state when all becomes still.

Then it becomes timeless. This is something that people will be given to experience for short periods of time as they are directed to do so. This is the concept of time and the concept of weather. It will be necessary to work for the harmony and balance within those interactions, for the big wind storms or snow storms are the result of Elementals not working in harmony with one another.

Question: "What is the cause of this disharmony?"

This comes through thoughts and how thoughts have been directed to these Elemental beings. The opportunity will be given to work with these beings, as they are here to assist you. Do you have any other questions?

Question: "I was just thinking what an adjustment that would be, where time would stand still for us. Does the new mathematics, dimensional mathematics, help us relate to those times?"

Most definitely, because there is no such thing as mathematics in a world of balance, for where would the pivot point or apex be, but at zero.

Question: "When the polar shift happens, will the Earth change its relationship to the moon or the sun and the orbits?"

Yes, again, because of the magnetism. Mankind needs to understand that these changes are for the Divine Good of all. It is necessary to bring harmony to the Earth and to integrate as ONE with the universe. The Earth is also part of a great Macrocosm and it must work in harmony with its other Brothers.

Question: "Will we be given similar information about other continents?"

America is a great focus of light for the Earth. They are the torchbearers, the people who hold great light for the rest of the world. Yes, there will be changes elsewhere but America will be the first to experience the changes and the first to overcome them and again hold the light. Look to your Higher Self at all times for the answers. Within the Higher Self is the Mastery of all things.

Saint Germain is sharing a new thought matrix or form to work with—it's an eight-sided shape.

9

*Recognize the spiritual energy present in
everything to create personal balance.*

Spiritual Structure

Last night Dan and I met at a local café where he shared some of his ideas concerning the Map and the idea of forming a business to publish and distribute the Spiritual Teachings. I can't help but be impressed by his enthusiasm and passion for the material, yet at times I feel reticent about sharing too much. He openly converses about the information with almost anyone—including his family, while I am a bit shy and worry what others will think. At this point, I've disclosed this information to only one trusted friend and our spiritual study group.

Dan has created an amazing logo, which contains the Dove of Peace—a symbol of one age ending and another beginning, and the five-stars as instructed from the Spiritual Teachers. "I AM America," Dan proudly announces as he hands me a black and white paste-up of the professionally designed graphic. The waiter asks for our order and I can tell Dan is selling me on the idea, and he orders two glasses of wine.

For the next hour he candidly shares his dreams for the publishing company: "Along with the Map, we can print a newsletter and then hopefully a book with the channelings!"

I recall that his sister once confided to me that she thought her brother a bit rash and at times a zealot about newly discovered ideas or lifestyles. My heart is pulled in two opposite directions: my need for privacy and carefulness versus Dan's purity, yet feral spontaneity—the latter qualities to which I'm obviously attracted.

The next day Saint Germain communicates his insights regarding the importance of Spiritual Structure.

Let's talk about structure. You've discussed the structure of your business. You've discussed the structure of the political system in the continent after changes. There is also the structure within, the spiritual structure.

Saint Germain is putting the words I AM on a chalk board. Alongside the "I," he is writing Intuition; alongside the "A," Armor; and alongside the "M" Me, myself.

Question: "How do I use this?"

I AM serves as the armor, the way of protection. Intuition is the focus for all that is good and is used for the path of the light. There are many ways you can use the intuition, depending on how you want to focus it and protect the structure of your intuition. The most simple, clearest way for spiritual growth is through the I AM, for it takes you to the heart of God.

Response: "This sounds like the most direct path."

The I AM is the clearest, the quickest, and the easiest. The I AM is a gift that has been given to mankind to lift and accelerate them in an easy, methodical way. You'll find the I AM constantly as a thread throughout many different cultures and religions. Everyone has their own way of relating to it and they will always have the right to choose whether or not they want the quickest way. The I AM is used at all different dimensional levels. Are there questions?

Question: "Would headaches have any relationship to the acceleration of vibration as we move the physical body toward Ascension?"

With three really bad headaches in the past few months around the temples and the left eye, I was wondering if these related to a misalignment.

The Third Eye Chakra can get misaligned when releasing unaligned energy in the form of a headache. It can be very painful at times but realize that there will come a time when that pain will cease. Specifically, send love and adoration to your Higher Self. Welcome the fact that you are releasing the energy from the misalignment and use the Violet Flame. We want to assist you but you need to ask. There have been times you haven't asked, but the times that you have asked, we have been there. When you feel energy coming through the top of the head, this is associated with the spiritual, the white cord.

Saint Germain is returning to the board and writing the word "Structure."

Concerning a misalignment and bringing it back into alignment, we can relate it to structure. When taking the simplest structure, you can always apply it to the larger structures and maintain the simplicity. If you picture a pyramid, at the lower levels, there is much more going on, more activity, more of everything. What makes it more complicated is that at these lower levels, it becomes more dense and takes on more energies. At each successive level, it becomes more simple, more streamlined, more directed and more focused. At the higher levels, it is similar to the top of the pyramid. Zero would be the apex, the point of balance. This is where we are. It is not the focus of nothing, it is the focus of all. Do you see this?

Response: "Yes."

So in your service, remember the concept of structure. Are there any other questions?

Question: "Is there more about the times zones that we need to put on the map?"

There are three time zones. With the Eastern Time Zone, the break comes in the Ohio Valley. With the Central Time Zone, the break comes almost to Denver. In the future, it will follow the mountain range. Then, the Coastal Time Zone is to the west.

Question: "About the weather crystal, when time stands still, can we still function and move around within that stillness?"

Absolutely. The body, while comprising Elemental Forces, is not of the elements. The true nature of man is his spirit. It is his Spirit which holds the elements together. When it all works in a cooperative fashion, this is true nature.

Question: "Will this stillness be over a large area of the region or just in a specific area, like the Ascension Valley?"

The stillness is directed through the Higher Self of the individuals who request it. We, as Ascended Masters, cannot interfere but the stillness is there for those to experience at their request. Much ground work is being laid now so that many will have this opportunity. That is what it is, a great opportunity.

Question: "And the people coming into this region for that experience, will that make Coeur d'Alene a transportation hub?"

A true corridor will exist there, but not only for transportation. There is also the Ascension Valley corridor. Transportation routes will just naturally open. There will be others, not naturally opened, but yet they will still become. Look at the correlation: Coeur d'Alene and corridor.

Question: "Will this be the only weather crystal in America and should it be protected?"

While it will originate here, it is a concept that can be used in other regions if a person or persons are willing to do so. The weather crystal is a sacred concept that has no mystery but should be protected.

Saint Germain has his arm around another Master and there are four of them and they all have their arms around one another, standing.

Let's talk about the structure of people and how we all help one another. How even at the ascended level, we cannot do what we do without the help and support of our own ascended Brothers.

10

Learning the benefits of teamwork.

Universal Energy

Saint Germain continues his lesson on how we all influence and affect one another. Sananda illustrates this important spiritual concept by appearing at Saint Germain's side. As they stand together, I feel the difference in the energy between the presence of one Master versus the two working together.

No doubt if Dan and I enter into this partnership, we will likely influence each other, both for good and for bad.

The energy of doing and helping is an energy of motion. This motion sets up a current, an electrical charge that is shared between the person you are doing something for and yourself. Both benefit from this current, as the energy goes to a higher level, or higher dimension, when it's shared by two people. If you were just by yourself and didn't have the opportunity to interact, it would be more difficult to take this energy and raise it. But by having others around you, you have this opportunity to raise energy.

Saint Germain is drawing a diagram of a spiral.

This spiral type of motion creates a pathway for attainment or Ascension. As the energy goes up, it is also freed into the universe, where not only you can draw upon it but others can draw upon it also. This is the concept of the universal. Universal is the motion of spiritual energy.

Next to Saint Germain is Jesus Sananda making a reference to a dove as his input and requesting that it be placed on the map as the symbol of one age merging into the next.

11

When to share, when to be quiet:
learning how to know.

Silence is Golden

Well Saint Germain finally addresses whether we should share this information, and if we do, with whom we should share it with. I am glad that Saint Germain is the one who finally addresses this issue and it is not left to me. Dan finally admits to Saint Germain that he knows that this is his "purpose," and that is why he is so talkative about the information. And he is normally a shy person! But how do you know when you are sincerely sharing or just proselytizing?

Question: "People have always been asked to keep this type of information silent in the past. Has this changed?"

Silence is golden. But what good is gold if the gold can't be used by the people. There is a time to be silent but there is also a time to be heard. Keeping silent about your inner work protects the inner thoughts that you have not yet manifested or integrated. Talking about things you haven't manifested gives the energy away and makes it harder to manifest what you are focused upon. But in this day and age, for something that is manifested and already brought into being, if you feel safe, give it out with your decree that it be for their higher good and Divine Path. Information, books and thoughts that are put into words, the silence is not as inevitable as the need to communicate.

The concept of the Higher Self and the current evolution of humanity—the Aryan—is still in spiritual conflict. The I AM has not been brought to mankind in its total form until now. You'll find it only in a few things and now is the time to find it in everything. Realize that you have a Divine Purpose and Path and will know intuitively what to say and what not to say.

There have been many other embodiments for all of us where we have lost our lives over our beliefs and the fear factor is a hard one to overcome but somewhere down the line, we need to eliminate the fear to open the channels. We live in a world of isolation in our silence and yet we also live a life of ignorance when we do not let it flow freely. Remember, it is the balance. Call to your Higher Self and say "Mighty I AM Presence, reveal the true inner nature of this person to me so that I may know the correct path to take." And then listen to your inner voice as it reveals something to you to let you know if it is right or not.

12

What is the purpose of the "deterioration" of a soceity?

Ancient Golden Times

I've found all the technical information incredibly boring, but I've remained patient, in hope of receiving specific insight to help my spiritual growth. After all, that is my main aspiration. After six sessions of dealing with mathematical calculations and specific mineral combinations—at last, a breakthrough with personal insights on a past-life with some explanation of the cycle of what seems like deterioration following Golden Ages.

Always look and listen for opportunities to put this information out. It's not only the opportunities but also the contact and the chance to meet people of like mind and energy. Are there questions today?

Question: "As you came through, I began remembering a past lifetime where we focused upon a Ray from the heart and one from the third eye to open up a channel of communication between us. Was this in Egypt?"

This was in Egypt, but it was early Egypt. You were Atlanteans living in the early Egyptian culture.

Question: "So, would this have been roughly around 8,000 years ago?"

That is correct.

Question: "What was our purpose then?"

You were in that culture to help raise it. You were not working particularly on spiritual aspects with people, but through education, fundamental mathematics, and the written word, which was the common teachings at that time. It was harder then to relate to the intermingling of cultures because each had a different religion. Atlanteans were known as the educators and you helped in the schools.

Theses schools were called the Temples of Enlightenment. You worked somewhat differently from one another, Lori with younger children, while you worked with older children. You taught them how to work with crafts and the Atlantean techniques of construction and science. I was your father then and a member of a democratic tribunal. In our own subculture, younger people helped to support the elders because they realized the true importance of keeping the spiritual culture growing. Eventually our culture deteriorated through intermarriages, yet it had been successful in raising the level of thought among the people. Do you have questions?

Question: "It seems like deterioration has happened after all the Golden Ages. Will that be the process again?"

It's a natural process. The Golden Ages are there to assist all upcoming and incoming souls. Golden Ages are a synthesis of the souls ready to transcend to other levels. The deterioration phase happens when the incoming souls are lifted and you have the dropping off of the number of people during that transition. While you view it as deterioration, it is actually a very natural part of the cycle of the upliftment. It allows a golden opportunity for all.

Question: "What did we learn at that time?"

You developed a level of patience that you had never had before, while Lori was a bit disappointed in that embodiment. She had set an unreasonable expectation but has since learned that expectation is not a necessary part of the process. Just doing is enough in itself.

13

Why are certain groups of people together?

The Descent

The idea of soul groups is introduced in the next selection. Apparently our meditation group is just more than a random association, and we are referred to by several different Spirit Teachers as the "Council of Thirteen." I agree that we seem to have a connection beyond the physical, and I am constantly amazed at our timely and meaningful relationships. This support and acceptance of our channeled work and the Earth Changes material is unconditional—something we've yet to seek from close friends or family members. And even though we thirteen members are at different levels of spiritual development, we are indelibly linked in our evolutionary process.

❦

Question: "Can you tell me more about the Spirit Guide White Water and the purpose of the group he is teaching?"

White Water is an Arapaho mystic. He has not gone through the process of Ascension but he is closely associated with and tied to the Elemental Life Forces. This is what the Council of Thirteen is about and your continuing work with that Council.

I was wondering if all thirteen of us were embodied at the same time then and if not, perhaps it would explain information received that we would not all meet at the same time now.

Question: "Does the Council deal with the Earth or Elemental activities for a region?"

Yes, and it was in the region of the Arapaho as an Indian culture. It also existed in pre-Atlantean days and helped form some of the foundations of spirituality that were brought into Atlantis. You were part of the beginning of the red race, although your physical embodiment was somewhat different than what you understand now. The

Council of Thirteen comprised not only people in actual physical embodiment but also those who had not fully developed physical bodies. These would be more on a Spirit Guide level or in a transition between the two and involved in the process of densifying their bodies.

People tend to think of taking on flesh as a carnal need but many of us took on the flesh out of a spiritual need. In the course of being in the flesh, we began to understand more of the carnal ways. This is what the Council of Thirteen is about, densifying into physical embodiment for spiritual, rather than carnal, need. While there is the upliftment of the animal aspects, there is also a descent. The Council of Thirteen worked for the descent.

When dealing with the Elementals in terms of densifying into a physical body, you are dealing with earth elements and a vast understanding of Elemental Forces. There is a difference between those who were already here and those who needed the teaching from a descent, from coming down to help. The Council of Thirteen was a manifestation from more of a Spirit Guide world.

Question: "What will be our purpose at this time? Is it to help with the transition into the New Age or understanding more of our relationship with the Elementals as the new Council of Thirteen?"

The specific purpose is to come to the knowledge of this again, bring it back, and close the circle. Realize that within the circle there is also the spiral. You are all at different levels of the spiral now. This is a wonderful thing that has happened, as in the descent, you were also all at different levels of understanding.

14

*The Earth Changes may cause animal
extinctions, and change in the human diet.*

The Animal Kingdom

Animals serve several purposes in our life. First, they comprise a major source of protein in our diet and are a major industry in our agricultural food system. Second, many animals are our pets and, according to Master Kuthumi, assist the evolution of the human emotional system. What affect will the changes have upon the Animal Kingdom?

Master Kuthumi addresses the topic of the human diet through his prophetic knowledge of the upcoming changes and the new sustainable agricultural practices of the future. This he shares alongside his knowledge of the possible extinction of certain species of animals, both domestic and wild. Raised on a farm, I admit I am a "meat and potatoes" gal! But lately I've been experimenting with vegetarianism and, I admit, I feel lighter and more connected spiritually. Is it possible that our diet is related to our spiritual development?

＊

I AM Kuthumi and have come to talk to you about the possible elimination of many animals from the physical during the Time of Change. There will not be the animal populations that you are used to having. These Elemental beings that are animals have been the expression of human emotion in many ways. People who have been around or close to animals have been refining certain characteristics about themselves and will soon no longer need to work on that. Also, many of you have used animals for food production and while this has never been the original intent for animals in interacting with human beings, it has served a purpose. During the Time of Change, one element that will come back more strongly because of the increase in water, particularly in this region, will be a lot more fish life and shellfish life. At the same time, there will be quite a bit less life as we perceive as animals. Do you have a question?

Question: "Wouldn't it take a while for the fish and shellfish to establish themselves in the waters?"

Yes, but you must understand that they are a more adaptable life force and the word again is cooperation. Presently, with man out of balance in the way that he is, the runs of fish life have been affected. There will be a period of time when this will continue to diminish. Then, we will have an adjustment as mankind becomes ready to work at finer levels.

Question: "Are there particular kinds of animals that will become extinct?"

It will be hard to sustain herds of cattle and to sustain horses. There will be some smaller animals that will be able to survive. The birds will still survive but the wilder beasts such as elk or bear will have a harder time. It is specific to the changes in the environments and the lack of food.

Question: "Would this be from a lack of sun and an excess amount of rain, that a lot of the plants will die before the transitional plants come in?"

Because of the lack of food and nourishment for these types of animals, it will not be possible for them to sustain their life force much longer. This brings a need for us to look at alternative foods, specifically aquaculture. Man also needs to look at his killing of creatures for his survival. Because of your great love for animals as part of the Elemental Force, I would like to give assistance and help if you would like to receive it.

Question: "Yes, very much. What would be a good start, in the aquaculture or in the areas of sprouting or growing under these adverse conditions?"

Man has the misconception that a high level of protein is essential in his diet. We all know this is not specifically true. These are things which will change and yes, aquaculture is the place to start to help with the transition. Man must also realize how he has misqualified his emotional needs to animals and how animals have qualified that back.

Question: "What kind of changes will our bodies be going through as we change our diet this radically?"

The changes are happening now. The higher level of spiritual energies which you are learning to filter is entering into your system. These are energies that have always been there and around you yet you have blocked them out. Now as you open up to them, you also must be open to the fact that the things that you eat also are the things that you become. So the culture of birds and aquaculture, the culture of fish, are two aspects which should be explored for Earth Changes. This has been happening already in an unconscious direction. Do you understand?

Response: "I think so, yes. I know in the last ten to twenty years there has been an increase in Idaho of raising trout on a large scale and also game birds."

They should be nurtured within the environment naturally. Particularly with an animal such as a bird in confinement or a food production environment, the disease factor is much higher. We'll need to look at the more Elemental races of this type of being.

15

*People in our corporate food systems need
to know what could happen.*

Food Storage
Saint Germain
Lady Opportunity

In an unpublished session, Saint Germain and Dan bantered about man's food sources and it was obvious that the spiritual guidance was not what Dan expected. Sometimes I feel caught in the middle of these spiritual arguments. This type of teaching—about something as basic as food—can evoke an inner conflict, and it is becoming more obvious that receiving and implementing this information is a growth process for both of us. Dan is learning how to trust. I am learning not to personalize the messages and just be the messenger!

On this topic I observe that my perception is changing. When in trance, I'm able to recognize the important subtleties and nuance of energy that accompany different types of Spirit Teachers.

In this session, The Master Teacher Lady Opportunity speaks about the importance of change in food storage, which implies almost a complete restructuring of our food systems in anticipation of possible Earth Change. She suggests to Dan that he can begin the process of finding the right people to work with through the spiritual practice of simplicity, focus, and requests to his Higher Self. I trust it is that easy.

My invocation at this time is somewhat different than the normal way of opening and Saint Germain is saying that it was well done because I am recognizing the different aspects of entities and people around us. White Water is a spiritual advisor, Mahani is my friend and Spirit Guide, Saint Germain is my sainted Master Teacher and of course, the mightiest of all within our own self and above ourselves is our own mighty I AM Presence, where the emphasis needs to be placed at all times. Saint Germain steps forward.

Question: "What information is necessary regarding food storage and finding someone to work on that area?"

This is one of the aspects you will be working with in service to the Green Ray, as food is related to health and health to healing. Food itself, the true foods that are green, are the ones that are the essence of health. Within chlorophyll is a crystalline gem structure. Find out the structure of chlorophyll as a thought matrix to focus upon for visualization. To find this person, go to your Higher Self and ask the Higher Self to set this into motion and into process. At any time if you need assistance, it will be there. There is a sainted Master present, Beloved Lady Opportunity, who would like to speak if you would like to listen.

Response: "Yes."

I will assist you in finding the right person along this line. This person or the network of people you need to find are those already in existing businesses. It will not be a matter of one person who will have all the knowledge. You need to find the people that are already in massive food production businesses and eventually, one person within your own organization to network, who can work easily with these large companies. This person would need to be willing to deal with many different personalities and yet be able to perceive within the personalities, the Oneness and search for God, for that is the quality which can assist us the most. There are many major food companies: General Foods, Del Monte, just to name a few and these all should be contacted. Within their structures are many people and there will be people within these structures to help and assist. Find the focus for your project and start your correspondence in a simple manner. Ask your Higher Self to bring these people to you.

Question: "So it is up to us to pick the focus first?"

Exactly, find your focus and the questions you need to write to these companies. Have one most simple issue in your mind at all times and I will be there to assist you. Remember I AM Lady Opportunity and I have served Earth for many ages. May I help you more?

Response: "That is fine for now."

16

What is sound?
What is time?

Sound
Saint Germain

I've noticed that my channeling style is integrating; that is, I no longer feel a disconnection between myself and the Spiritual Teachers. Months ago when I first started with this work, this spiritual communication was much like a telephone. I could hear conversations on either side of the ethereal dimension—Saint Germain's insights and Dan's questions. Now this process is seamless. Once I enter into the trance-state, I sense a feeling or sound almost like a physical, "Tap . . . tap." And then my consciousness literally becomes ONE with the Spiritual Teacher. Saint Germain explains why.

Question: "About time and sound, you were saying that sound has a wave, and time is parallel. Does that mean that time is not energy, since it does not have a wave?"

Time is a perception. Time is only a measurement which we use at this moment to understand. It is a perceptual wave. This is a principle of interdimensional mathematics, perceptual waves. Sound is a principle of the God element of all elements. There is sound which keeps molecules together. Time is perceptual. What is time to one is not time to another. Yet, it does exist and yet it is only one's perception of how it exists.

Question: "Is there a way of working with the waves of sound or other energies that would alter time?"

Yes, there are and your enthusiasm is wonderful. Where should we start?

Question: "If my thoughts were at the right vibrational frequency, where I was only picking up on the highs of the sound waves, would that alter the time differently than if I were picking up on the low waves?"

Your perception of highs and lows is the key. Intermingled within the Law of Sound are also again the perceptual waves. Mastery of the perceptual waves is the Mastery of sound and the Mastery of time together. There are the clear notes of God, the clear notes of the I AM, and the clear notes of the universal that are indeed timeless. There is perception of arrangement of the clear note. Yes, there are sounds that are timeless. And yes, you can travel on these sounds.

Question: "My limitations now are limitations of my hearing or perception of sound?"

Yes, sound is no more than a Vibration of the Universe. We are talking of Elemental Forces. Sound is interwoven in between the Elemental Forces but sound and light are also the two waves which travel directly out of the physical and into other realms of manifestation. While the wind is not present in other realms, sound and light are and yet there are other realms where sound does not exist. Are you confused?

Response: "No, I just don't know where to start."

You may start by finding the true note, the true notes that have been used throughout the centuries. Understand the process, understand the rhythm of arrangement. Listen to the elements and you will hear the sounds woven throughout them.

17

*In every situation and circumstance,
we are spiritually evolving and growing.*

Everlasting Wholeness
Higher Self
The Grand One
Saint Germain
Lady Opportunity

Dan openly admits his fear that, through my channeled sessions, I may become too much of a crutch for him and inhibit his own ability to develop spiritually. It is apparent that the more that I develop my ability to channel, the more it seems to invite Dan's insecurities.

Even if we can't paint a Picasso, sing opera like Domingo, or in this case channel Ascended Masters, we all have our unique talents and abilities that cannot be overlooked. The Great White Brotherhood seeks students with diverse talents, from every walk of life.

❧

I opened up the channel just to my Higher Self and we're walking in a garden and she has plucked an orange from a tree. She cut it open and is showing me the individual sections inside, saying that I need to remember at all times, that while I have so many parts of my life going on, that each section is still part of the whole. Now she's taking me to a place to understand how to sustain wholeness and joy in living. It's brilliant, there's a gold floor and a gold warm light all around. It feels sort of like a platform. I'm standing in such a way that each side looks like a point on a star.

This is a place you can go to feel your wholeness as part of the ONE. Feel yourself to be a gold star, as well as all the others. You have a place, purpose and direction. Is there any particular thing you wanted to ask?

Question: "Yes, sometimes when I ask for help it comes in right away and other times, it feels like nothing happens. Why is this?"

Of your abilities, one of them is that you are very quick. In fact, you were once a runner and you would run between towns and give messages. Often times, you are too quick and you don't slow down and see what the problem is. Yes, there are times when it comes to you really in a direct way because of your expedient methods. There are other times when you need to slow down to catch the finer details. Do you see this?

Response: "Yes, but I am concerned that I will not develop my own abilities assisting Lori."

Your abilities are there, but you need to slow down. Your abilities are developing anyway and you feel it and it makes you want to go faster at times, but slow yourself down. Find the things that help you to slow down. When you do slow down, realize that you are doing this for a Divine Purpose and that it has meaning and value far more than anything else you can do at this moment. Do you understand this?

Response: "I think I do, but I get impatient."

You have a need to justify everything and since that is the way your mind has a tendency to function, it's okay to take the time to slow down because there is a reason that you're doing it. You are not impatient so much as your mind is quick. It moves far ahead sometimes even of your physical body. But at times you need to slow down in order to feel the other substances around you. Even if you only use your intellect at this moment, slow it down. Do you see yourself as the runner? Do you remember yourself as the runner?

Response: "No, but I used to have a very euphoric feeling when I was younger running through the forest like a deer."

Well, remember when you did run for others, you would push yourself…that pushing isn't necessarily the method here. To be inspired is one thing but to push yourself unnecessarily, again, does harm to yourself. You are beginning to understand this. If you have no other question, there is someone else here for you. He is a teacher. You have been in contact with him all through the ages and he is very special to you. His name is the Grand One. He would like to talk to you about time. He wonders if you remember tearing apart a clock at one time? Do you want to talk to him?

Response: "Yes, I tore apart several clocks when I was younger."

In tearing apart those clocks, what was it that you discovered about the clock?

Response: "I don't remember my thoughts at that time."

Inside were the tightly wound springs that were coiled and in a way, it seemed as though this could not really be the concept of time to you...that time is only a spring. This is when I was contacting you and working with you to help you to understand that it is okay to be yourself, to be who you are. And I'm glad to see that now you've come to know this and that you have taken the time to look within. I would like to work with you again, personally, if you would permit me.

Response: "I would love it."

When you want to contact me in your meditations, look for my face and remember the clock. This will be the symbol between us. I will hand you the clock. You are ready for initiation and do not hold back. I will be with you always.

Question: "What do you mean by initiation?"

The steps to enlightenment, to fundamental knowledge, are inner truths that are shared at inner levels. You witnessed my Ascension as the runner and you didn't understand at the time when you saw it but you have continued to push and I have stayed with you always. Now I will help you so you may witness your own.

Saint Germain steps forward.

I am concerned that you are not using the Violet Flame enough. It is essential that you continue to use it and to not stay away from that path and direction. It is the gift of this age. It is yours to use freely at all times.

He has placed his hand on each of our foreheads and a Violet Flame has come from his hand and is covering us from the top of our heads on down. He's reminding us to continue to use this at all times.

Response: "Boy, I just felt like I was floating...I felt something different!"

I felt something different too. It felt like my link up with my own Higher Self was more intense. I'm at the portal of communication and they're saying now I can truly feel all of them and they are asking if I can feel it as a circle of light around me. I could feel this and it was different this time than any other time I've done this. This must be the same tube of light I had been reading about.

Question: "I was reading the second Law of Thermodynamics, which states that systems left to themselves run down and the macroscopic properties that describe them become independent of time. It seems to me that our culture's concept of the beginning of everything is a void or stillness, so that we believe that everything dissipates back to nothingness. I was thinking, what if we could change our beliefs to the beginning being everything, all energy, the highest vibrational rate of God's Source? Would we then be able to change our belief to everything left alone, not isolated but left alone, would naturally increase its energy or vibrational rate until it reached the highest or the God source?"

I'm glad that you found the book I recommended to you. This reading will assist you greatly in the next five years. And congratulations, you've just crossed another threshold in understanding realities of universal principle and law. This is the biggest misconception mankind has, not believing until they see. Yet it's been the only way man has been able to function with an element of reason in the physical. Not to believe in the fire until he sees the fire, or the water until he sees the water.

In this instance, we are dealing with the unseen forces. For instance, the wind, do we see the wind? But we feel the wind and we see the effect of the wind. We see it in patterns over the globe and yet do we see it when it blows in the air? No, we don't. There are these things which we must learn to see and feel and to measure. This is the concept of interdimensional mathematics, bringing the spiritual forces into mathematical play in the physical. For there are those who will never come to a level of acceptance until these principles are manifest. This is the time to do so for the great cleansing of Earth.

Response: "When others watch someone reach their Ascension, this will help them to believe in these spiritual concepts."

Absolutely. These principles of thermodynamics and interdimensional mathematics will work in a harmonious way with all those involved. They will work in a way not only integrating into their projects, but into their plans, into their lives, and into their being. It is a whole unit separate to itself and also part of all. I'm holding my right hand to you; will you grab it and walk with me and join our Brotherhood?

Response: "Yes."

Welcome, this is the link which we need. We need to have people who will earnestly seek, who will earnestly work, and earnestly help in all capacities to bring this to fruition. Do you know the sign of the Brotherhood?

Response: "No."

Your hand to your heart, to your third eye, and then above. This is a symbol brought to the physical level as the symbol of the trinity. All those who will help you and assist you will be contacted by the Brotherhood. This symbol is the dance of the flame, and the circle of the flame from which we all take great joy. The most current one in your culture who has studied this and where there is a written record is Saint Francis, although the American Indian, in their culture, understood this too and you may find bits and pieces in their culture as well.

Question: "There is a book from the Mount Shasta group on initiation. Will that help?"

Yes, they will help. Realize that the Brotherhood is releasing information on many levels but it is the recognition of the Brotherhood and the recognition of our cooperation together that is the principle at work here. I'm glad that you've recognized this. Your symbol from one embodiment as an American Indian was the turtle. It has to do with everlasting life and the symbol is around you presently and you must understand this. Are you seeing yourself and your life now more as a total unit?

Response: "Yes, definitely. I realized a purpose and direction."

So this is the reason you will continue on this map. Earth is a total and whole entity, a being unto herself, and this is the total purpose of the map. People must come to terms with this. They cannot see it as something that they just function upon. They must see it as a total and living organism, whole and to itself. This is the principle of the turtle. Not just with the American Indian; you will find it as well in the Oriental cultures and although we use the symbol of the turtle, the concept is everlasting wholeness. Now the Goddess of Opportunity is here to help you on the food issues and would like to know if you have a plan for a network?

Response: "No, I don't, I've just been concentrating on getting the map out and keeping my business going right now. I haven't given it much thought yet."

Your business is the opportunity for growth at this period. It is blessed and you are as well. Remember that it always will give you what you need at all times. Look upon the map itself, which has been brought to manifestation. See the cities and set up the network from the major food companies. Do you understand what I'm saying? With massive changes ahead, it would be senseless to set up a food source from the California coast. It would be senseless to set up a food source from Seattle. Get your contacts. Prepare and be ready. Set up your contacts from those places which will remain. Remember the climates. Remember the massive changes. There are protected areas. Seek them out and find them. Those are the ones to network with. Trust that they will be there. Trust that they will help you.

Response: "Yes, I do believe that but my biggest hang up right now is more a lack of money to travel, to do things, to put things in process."

You have no lack, for all that you need is there at any moment for you to use. Do you believe this effort is foolish?

Response: "No, not at all."

Do you believe this effort is harming another?

Response: "No."

Do you believe this effort is harming yourself?

Response: "No."

Then you have passed all criteria of cosmic law. What you need will be there. You must trust this. I will assist you and help you in these manners. I will work with you and help to attract the people to you who need to help you. This is an effort you must not do alone. This is an effort you must do together with cooperation and opportunity for all to participate.

Remember at all times to make your weakness your highest shining quality. Say at all times, "I AM opportunity, I AM all that I need at all times." I understand your reservations about time but this too will come into balance. I must leave now and turn the floor back to Saint Germain.

I would prefer now to talk about the Violet Flame and the use of it on a daily basis. Are you doing so?

Response: "Yes."

Make your calls at times where you can totally silence and quiet yourself. When you make your call for the Violet Flame, close your eyes and see it flowing and burning up all through and around you. Its cleansing action is invigorating and will help you in your efforts. Its effect is incredible.

18

Dealing with financial fears.

Travels with the Master
Saint Germain

Dan's financial pressures increase. A large business debt, well over fifteen thousand dollars, looms alongside the need to find the necessary funding to print and market the Map. Interestingly, the Master Teachers are still encouraging, and it is important to note that while they do not "tell us" exactly what to do, they offer advice and spiritual techniques to improve this temporary financial situation. It is apparent that as we embrace their spiritual tutelage, we still have our own unique karmas to resolve. And no doubt, one of Dan's life lessons centers around money and his ability to manifest and manage it. This lesson offers a visualization and meditation to release fear, and how to prepare your spiritual consciousness to overcome neediness. According to Saint Germain, if done as he has instructed, this can produce a miracle. At this point, a miracle is in order!

❧

After a series of decrees, we are in the center of the Circle of the Violet Flame. Saint Germain is dressed differently today, in a violet robe with gold trim on the sleeves. He's handing me one to put on too and then holds out his hand to me. We're going to an inner retreat, one of his retreats in Transylvania, which almost looks like a medieval castle. He thought I would enjoy this because I had been there before. We're walking down a hall with portraits on both sides. The floor is a glossy type of stone. We're stopping in front of one portrait of a man from the eighteenth century. Saint Germain indicates that this man is currently in embodiment again and is a great scientist. We're walking into a dining area.

At times great councils come and meet here at the table. Do you have any questions that you want to ask while we're here? We can walk through all the rooms if you want to.

Question: "That's fine. Is this building in the physical dimension?"

It is in the physical but cloaked. There is no way to see it now but there was a time when you would visit here. This was my base of operation during the French period, working for the consolidation of Europe. It is still a place of rest where I go, a place where you are welcome. The Maltese Cross I AM wearing over my heart, I would like you to use as visualization for transformation and in any trying situation. Picture the Maltese Cross over your heart and call for the higher good of any situation and it will transform your lives.

Saint Germain has something he wants to show you. He's pulling a sword down and thought that you would remember it. It is encrusted with jewels on one side, though they had been added later. There is something about the sword, some sort of symbol.

You helped in making the sword when you worked with me when I was Merlin. It was a special type of metal in the sword and it was, as you understood at that time, the electrical currents that run through our bodies that this metal would respond to. That is how the sword was able to be pulled. The story is very true and also has a deeper symbology, of being planted firmly in God. Being able to pull others to God is part of the symbol.

Now he's showing me two saddle bags that fit over the sides of a horse and inside he's pulled out pouches. Inside the pouches are gems. He's placed three in my hand and closed my hand around them, a diamond, an amethyst, and an emerald. The diamond is my stone, the emerald is yours. The amethyst is the transformation stone and a stone of union, the union of the self to the Higher Self. The energy is incredible. I'm giving them back to him now. When I first saw the pouches, I remembered seeing these someplace before.

Question: "Why are they in saddle bags?"

So you would remember how these came to you once in the desert. I'm showing you these because sometimes we seem barren, we seem fruitless, we seem to have no purpose and yet suddenly from this barrenness comes the highest vibration, the highest thing, a shining stone of priceless value. Now do you remember?

I remember being camped out on the desert and these riders coming and unloading their bags and showing these to me. They would take these stones at night and set them up like the constellations. I remember wondering where these riders had come from. I worked with gold, making jewelry just out of metal, gold bracelets and earrings. I felt very isolated. I wondered why?

I am showing you this today to help you let go of fears.

He wants you to hold your hand out and he's placing the green stone, an eight-sided emerald, into it.

This is the highest you can do for financial concerns—meditate. This is your meditation:

> I AM fruitful, I AM full of peace, I AM all that I need from the universe
> at all times. I AM creating this day for opulence and abundance. I AM
> ONE with God and God is ONE with me, the Almighty I AM Presence.

With this visualization, remember that every need you have will be met accordingly. This you must do and do it, if not on a daily basis, three to nine times a day. As well as for yourself, do it for the people surrounding these money issues as well. Do it for all your business partners and associates. Do it for members of your family. Do this all in accordance with the Divine Plan. Always call to the I AM and these issues will dissolve in front of you. When you say the decree, simply put their name in the place where you normally would see your name. Start this immediately, for yourself and those around you and it will work a miracle.

19

What changes? What stays the same?
Does one affect the other?

Portals

The following lesson is another mind-expanding session on how the underlying principles of science blend with certain aspects of spiritual development. The idea of spiritual silence, or emptiness, is mirrored in what Saint Germain explains as the *Theory of the Void*. Since these sessions often deal with new knowledge and information we've never before encountered, they are intense and often require periods of solitude in order to integrate their vital importance into our personal and spiritual growth. The Master Teacher reiterates that this process leads to profound change that is both a natural process and a "continual life process." Reminds me of the Hermetic Philosophy, "As above, so below; as within, so without." We are constantly reflecting, recognizing, and expanding the inner change engendered in our spiritual consciousness.

We have a lot of work to do today and Saint Germain has shown me a new way to open up my direct link with him, which is even more focused and quicker. I visualize the Maltese Cross right over my heart and then see it on his and it is an instantaneous connection. He is in front of the chalkboard writing about mathematical principles of thermodynamics.

I would like to explain the Theory of the Void, for within understanding this theory, man will come to understand the scientific and mathematical principles applying to the unseen worlds. Voids help to create the gateway to another dimension. Mankind has studied some of the theories of voids to understand what a black hole is and yet missed the true principle altogether. This is the way for interstellar communication. It is possible, that in understanding thermodynamics and interdimensional mathematics, we can open the door for these levels of communication. This can occur not only with other life forms on other planets but also for the Time of Change, so that we have the open communication that will be needed. For all of these things are part of the whole and assist, aid and help each other.

Saint German is drawing a circle just inside another circle and a dot in the middle. He is making a dimensional shape by projecting a cone shape from the bottom and another cone shape from the top. He takes both of the cones and breaks them apart. There's a swirling action inside the cones.

The swirling action forces energy to the outside of the cone. In the inside is this concept of the void, yet this is where the highest concentration is, always in the core. So you have this action on both sides of the dimensional. What happens on the inside of this perceptual space is a shape which flows within itself, is self contained. This energy that is self contained is the principle of that within the circle. If you were to find the true center point of all of the energy, the consolidation of this energy, it would go to the circle with the dot. At both ends of this dimensional shape are where the electrical currents run and these are the points where we can tap into this kind of energy.

As the energy circles around toward the outside, it slows down into more of a substance form and that's where we perceive it here, in this dimension. As this energy is swirling within the cone, the highest energy, the most vibration, is in the center core and as it swirls around towards the outside, it slows down its rate. These are also the positions where we can enter into that dimension and we tap into, though unconsciously, through meditation. When you understand these principles, you can physically walk into that dimension.

Communication is the same thing, as the barrier that exists between men is a wrong perception. Through entering into this source, we will find more simple ways to communicate and still give the messages that are needed. Is this not the process of simplification, discarding the human elements that you have discovered do not work for you anymore? This is the new form of communication and interstellar communication.

Question: "A lady I met in the Reiki workshop this weekend is receiving channeled information. She is helping people get food and healing information together and mentioned communication between the protected areas by means of telepathy during the Time of Change. Is this related to the information that we're receiving this morning?"

Yes, it is. This is one area which needs development.

Question: "Is this something we should start practicing with our friends who are moving to the Southwest?"

Yes, and within your map, you will find the areas with this shape. You will be able to pinpoint the portals. Draw this out dimensionally and you will see intuitively where to place them. You will discover these points.

Question: "Would the poles be Vortex areas, portals of the Earth?"

Right… portals, this is the concept used when people are led to different portals of magnetism throughout the Earth. Remember how we opened up our portal of communication originally, through love and appreciation. Now we have refined it one step further, to a visualization based upon these principles of love. Remember that it is the same when you open up a portal to this organism, this living being that is Earth. It is built on the same principles of communication and love and then taken through higher perspectives.

Question: "Am I right in assuming that the different veins of ore are like the nerves that are recharging the energy in the core of Earth from the cosmos?"

Very similar to your physical body, yes, this is the same concept of absorbing energy from the universe, from the sun and also within the atmosphere itself. All of these portals are interconnected with these capillaries of Earth. Gold carries the highest energy and then silver. There are also the gem deposits which give clarity to purpose. The diamond is the highest.

Question: "What about the quartz material we found on a friend's property?"

This was an ore which was quite common. It was fused to the stone through an electrical process. It had the effect of absorbing like the capillaries or veins of Earth absorb sunlight in the atmosphere. It was used in construction of many of the retreats. Though man-made, it was built upon principles of Earth.

Question: "Is that the black and red material that is finely distributed around the crystal and adhering to it?"

Yes and these types of ores originated from the beginning of the red race.

Question: "Are these portals still used or are there new ones being created for the new energies?"

While the structure remains the same, the magnetism can change upon occasion. But the general structure remains the same. Remember, as above so below. Also remember the concept of the mirror. Look at your physical body itself: have your ears changed or your nose? No. Have the poles ever changed? They still have North, they still have South. There is structure that always remains the same, although some arrangement and dimension could be different. This we know from the way Earth has changed through the eons and also how you have changed your physical body through the eons.

Question: "In modeling this to our personal selves, in placing the circle on top of the head, with the crown chakra at the center, does this create a Vortex down through our solar-spinal cord from the focus of our Higher Selves?"

This is an energy Vortex that is already in place. It is the structure again that is within.

Question: "Would it be helpful to visualize this in our meditations?"

Oh, yes, it is good to be aware of all of the energy forces which comprise your own energy field.

Question: "As the core of Earth spins in its centrifugal motion, throwing the energy toward the outside, I am assuming the energy loses its vibrational rate and becomes the physical shell of Earth?"

Yes, you have the concept down. The spinning of the spiritual energy and the interaction with the elements create this physical shell or casing around the spiritual energy.

Question: "Are there individual spiritual entities within Earth that manifest as the Elementals on the surface or are there different levels of beings?"

Yes, there are Elemental Forces which could live there and do indeed travel to the center of Earth. They are the higher perspective of the Elementals, the guiding force behind that which has manifested. It is a place where the consciousness of many dwell. It is a place where many could live. It takes on new properties, for it is the spinning action of the spiritual and, to the outside again, is manifested the physical.

Question: "So, would it be a similar process with our human form, where we have the sperm and egg and the life force spinning and manifesting our form over a period of time?"

Precisely, and observe the shapes. The egg is round. Look at the shape of the sperm with its cone shape. Do you see this?

Question: "Yes. Some instruments pick up a lot of energy coming in from the cosmos. I was also wondering about how Earth absorbs energies and where these other energies are coming from?"

There are other galaxies which emit energy to Earth. Every planet within your solar system sends a quality that Earth absorbs or reflects in accordance to her needs. For you are the same way; you have many people within your inner group, metaphorically within your solar system, and yet there are others within your community. Do you accept the energies from all these people? No, you don't, but yet you accept the energies from some, those which nurture you, those which give you what you need.

Earth is much the same way; she and he together work as a living organism. Many people have modeled this concept of the "she and he" as the Mother Earth and the Father Sun but both of these qualities are inherent within Earth itself. For you can see Earth nurtures, Earth must protect itself as well. The Divine Compliment of Mother Earth is also the Father image, the protector of what is. The sun also has both its female and male qualities.

Question: "The large solar flare ups that have happened recently, how is that affecting Earth? Is that part of Earth's changing process?"

It will have ramification on Earth. Are we not in the Aquarian Age and have we not said that this is the Time of Change? Do not fear, fear is not the purpose, but you know this already. It is interconnected, for as the Earth Changes, so does the solar system and so does the Galaxy. Remember, as you change, do not the people around you change as well and does not the community also change from the impact of your circle of friends who have changed? This is the continual life process. It is natural and it is complete and yet it has purpose and Divinity within it.

20

Honing our communication skills.

Three Coins
Higher Self
Saint Germain

I've been channeling for about three months now and I still feel a bit of discomfort with my newfound abilities. In this lesson, I learned the anatomy of communication—through my body and integration with the Higher Self and the I AM Presence. The three coins mentioned in this selection are symbols of a form of psychic work I performed for others in another lifetime. Now that I am mastering trance work, these coins take on a new meaning. This lesson shares insight on communicating through the I AM Presence.

I called for the Violet Flame to surround me and I shot up through the cord, where my Higher Self is handing me clothing. First, sandals and then a dress to put on and a ring. She wants me to use this for a visualization, to remind me that I am surrounded at all times by the I AM Presence and my Higher Self. I can put these on at any time to be ONE with the Source. Then she is handing me three gold coins that were symbols I once worked with to do readings of sorts for people. These coins seem to have taken on a higher meaning for me now. She wants me to live in the joy and peace that I AM. Saint Germain steps forward.

Greetings. You are beginning to start the work that you came here to do. You are getting more ready to do the things that need to be done. Your emphasis will be working with people and bringing them the message of the love and joy of I AM. You will help them to see the true nature of this message. Remember, when you did the readings with these coins, you focused more on the higher intellect. Now, you will have the opportunity to go one step further, beyond the intellect.

Saint Germain has drawn a circle with a point in the middle and square around the point. He puts another square offset a little bit and then others, so that they spiral around the center. The exact center point of this energy is the highest densification of energy. Within the spiral is a core spiral, the passageway of the portal. It looks similar to a spiral staircase, yet it is more of a square. He's writing next to it C /R.

This is a distance to time ratio, "C" being communication and "R," radius. So the communication issue is really a matter of distance and time. Visualize yourself standing over this circle. Within the circle is the larger portion of the spiral and through the top of the head is the center. When the spiral extends out through the body through the lowest chakra, if your legs are slightly apart, you can see another pyramid shape forming in the lower quadrant. Now, see the core spiral within the larger spiral as the energy Vortex of the spinal column with the nerve endings. Even though there are other energies around us, this cord is important, for from this cord comes all other perceptions. This has a measurable wave and once you learn to measure it, you will understand it better and be able to listen through it and to speak through it. When learning to measure and speak through this cord, you will then go one step further, to manifest through speech. Manifestation is another principle of this portal.

If you look at a piece of clear quartz, you will understand that it has a similar structure and wavelength to our nervous system. It too wants to be a pure vessel, to contain and reflect the white light. This too is our purpose in our physical densification. In the center of the crystal's molecular structure is the same principle, two spirals, the one within the two forming the portal and means to communicate. Again, the spatial distance is the communication to the radius, distance and time, two over one, one over two.

Now he has in front of me a black six-sided cube. He's cut it in half and to the center is a round ball. He's cut it in half again and inside of the round ball is again the cube. Two in the one, one in the two. Now he's putting it back together and twisting one of the halves. He's showing again this same principle, how it works. At the top of both sides he's put a silver plug of some sort. And down through the center, a rod of some nature. And as the rod goes through the portal in the center, it disappears and yet comes out the other end. You can still see the ends, but as it reaches the center, the rod which is seemingly there, is not there.

This is the theory of trans-galactic communication.

21

Learning to find quality amidst fear.

Communication

It has been ten days since Dan was given the meditation and decree technique for his money situation, and so far not much has changed. No doubt, this healing process will take some time for him, and I feel worry and a deep compassion for his situation! In this lesson, Saint Germain reminds us that it is important to have a childlike innocence in trying situations, and this evokes the self-trust and joy that financial stress often wears thin. This lesson ends with visualization for simplicity and balance in seemingly complex circumstances.

Saint Germain is holding out his hand and three beams of light emerge, forming a triangle, two beams of light going out and the other one across. He is tipping it up and then he stands inside of it.

This process is potentially an accurate one. It is a way you can visualize portals for communication. A communication network, using this triangle, will have a common visualization that everyone can see to more or less tap into the telepathic line.

Question: "Does this triangle become a three-sided pyramid, a tetrahedron of energy?"

Yes, because when two people are communicating, it creates a third consciousness born of the two, which then becomes the ONE. Do you have any personal questions?

Question: "I've been keeping a journal that doesn't have much in it and I really haven't seen any direction or where to go. Why is this?"

Direction is qualified energy. Are you having trouble with feeling quality?

Response: "Yes. I'm sure I am."

Look for the small things. Take it one day at a time. In the present, find the small things each day that bring quality to you. This is not then directed motion. The smaller things which have this qualification give your life a sense of purpose and direction. Do you understand?

Response: "Yes, it's just that it's slow building from the small to get to the large positive energies."

Remember in the Bible, it says, "the meek shall inherit the Kingdom." If you don't become like a small child again, how will this process work? Open yourself up to the world of the child again. This time of discovery for you can be like taking a flashlight under a blanket and in the small little world, you are able to see with much more clarity the smaller things contained in that smaller world. Again, take this light into your life and examine everything closely for what it truly is. Do you understand this?

Question: "Well, I think so. I've probably been so down on myself that nothing seems to be working that I try. I'm bringing a lot of negativity into myself. Is that why my business just keeps getting worse and worse with nothing coming in?"

Remember that your business is a reflection of your energy and how your energy manifests in the physical through your actions. You qualify this energy through your actions. Now, take your directed energy, this energy we've been speaking about and direct it with a motive, a motive that is childlike, a motive that trusts, a motive that doesn't fear, a motive that is in the present. You think to yourself, what about my long-term goals, and yes, you may set those as well, but set them with the same childlike ways doing the things which bring you joy, doing the things which bring you more trust, doing the things that day by day take away the fear. And day by day, work with the Violet Flame.

Opulence and abundance are there for you at any time. Any time it is there for you. The difference is the perception. You perceive your opulence coming to you in such a way and yet it will come to you in any way when fear is taken away. Remember being a child again. Try hard to be this child, for it will set you free. Take the chain off the door, the door of your being, for becoming this child, you will know your true self. The true self is the Co-creator. In your wisdom, you've known this before. It is harder to recall the things we have forgotten without being reminded. How far do you want to continue with the personal lesson?

Question: "That's fine. What project do you suggest we work on?"

The Weather Vortex (crystal), for again this was the visualization of communication. In setting up this network, we'll be closely tied to weather vortices. Electromagnetism in the air can be of much benefit. And how is this produced? Through the elements. And yet, are not the elements directed and a reflection of the feeling mind of man? And so, working with the principles of electromagnetism, a new world can open up, a new visionary world through which we can create these portals to communicate. Inside, you find a shape in these electro-currents, the shape of the dextraphine. This is a crystalline star shape which rotates and spins, creating a force within the force. I will break this down so you may see it.

He's putting a number on the board, it's 44.

This number is associated with the number of points on this crystalline molecular structure. The shapes all fit together in perfect harmony and the force of their spinning creates a wholeness spinning within themselves and also a motion of itself as ONE. From each point comes a new current of energy. On one side the positive moves through to the neutral center and through to the other side, negative. Each point alternates, creating perfect balance in an unadulterated environment. However, as we direct our energies with the directive motives we have spoken about; the points of each of these become guided and misdirected. One structure will be charged one way and one, another way, instead of being in balance. When the 44 points are in balance, there is a current which forms the energy from which I speak. You may use thought into and upon this structure and when you understand this shape, you will then open up this portal. It is really quite simple and only complex to those who wish it to be. This is the principle for projecting our energies into the universe.

22

*Earth shifts parallel personal shifts: the inside
change evolves into an outer one.*

Earth Shift

About a week before our first formal presentation of the Map, Dan and I decide
to end our relationship. This leaves so many unanswered questions: what about
the Map project, who will give the presentation, and, above all, if I am to continue
channeling, who will facilitate the sessions? But the most overwhelming question is
one I must answer myself: "Do I want to continue with my trance work?"

In order to seek clarity, I decide to take a break from trance work, from seeing
Dan, and from working on anything associated with I AM America.

I ask Dan to handle the presentation, and since I was unsure if I will even
continue in any capacity with the Map, I ask him to protect my anonymity.
Although he agrees, I feel a great inner void.

I turn to traditional counseling, and try my best to explain my experiences with
the Map to a psychologist—he looks at me like I've totally lost it. One night, feeling
particularly down and hovering on despair, I sense a benevolent presence. I recognize
the Ascended Master Mary. I close my eyes and her energies blanket me in a field
of unconditional love. Her vibration lifts me out of my physical body and into a
state of consciousness almost similar to a trance state. She affirms, "I will take this
loneliness from you." And in this ethereal state, a spiritual darkness lifts from me,
which to this day has never returned.

No doubt, this healing is profound. Yet I still question my life's purpose. I buy a
mountain bike and ride the trail system that borders the Snake River levee system.
As I ride, I often enter into a dialogue with the River. "Show me my purpose," I
repeat to her slow-moving, dark waters. "Use me; let me serve," I plead.

I get the idea that if I sell my house, there will be more than enough money
to print and market the Map. I mention this to my counselor, and he warns me,

"Owning your home is a lot of security for a single mother." Nevertheless, I call the realtor who sold me the home during my divorce, and in twenty-four hours, my house is sold!

I have no idea how to handle Dan, and if we should continue in any type of relationship, especially with his financial pressure. A good friend advises, "When you pray, consider turning your relationship with Dan over to God," and this is what I do. I sincerely want healing between us; if we continue our spiritual work and print the Map, we'll need to reconcile at so many levels!

During this period, I feel the Presence ever so close and my spiritual connection with the I AM integrating—at times gently and subtly and sometimes furiously shifting and correlating energies and frequencies physically, mentally, and emotionally.

After a six month break, Dan and I reunite and, not surprisingly, we receive this lesson on consciousness shift. This describes the process of the growth of our spiritual light and how each individual influences the collective consciousness. The Earth mirrors this spiritual process and her inner light is also evolving and growing, and this continuous, natural process is unique and important at this time.

≈

Saint Germain is taking the globe and splitting it in half. You can see a second, inner globe and where the axis runs through and crosses the inner core.

The shift happens first. Within the inner core first within the very center, there is no gravity at all and the laws of gravity become void. As you go to the outer, it becomes more dense and we come more into the physical laws. This is a natural progression from the inside to the outer. Outer changes occur because a change has already happened within this inner part of Earth. There is a brilliant, brilliant white light in the center of Earth. This is a change that happened some time ago but is now ready to be brought to the surface. The actual shifting is this process of bringing this white core to this second inner globe that I am showing here. This is a timing device which affects the entire Earth. This is the third time, with this cosmic-type clock, that this has happened to the Earth, once during Atlantis and once for a civilization preceding Lemuria. This is a natural process, a necessary process.

Question: "Even though this has happened before, isn't this different because Earth is going through a change which parallels our spiritual growth and Ascension?"

Yes, as the human soul has evolved, we have had many opportunities and gone through similar processes. This is also a process for Earth itself. It's the bringing of the inner to the outer and then to a balance and alignment. The light within must have the opportunity to be directed to the outer, the same as within ourselves. We must learn to trust our light within and to share it with others. This is the same process that is happening here, a very natural process, a process of life, and the continuing of life.

23

Who is helping the Earth Change?

Twelve Brothers

Apparently there are many different types of spiritual teachers and guides assisting humanity to spiritually grow and evolve. Many are Ascended Masters and others are spiritual teachers from other planets and solar systems. This selection introduces the brotherhood of spiritual helpers, and their diverse work for humanity and on Earth.

Question: "I have read that the fallen angels and some of the negative Spirit entities have been cleansed from the ethers around Earth. Is this part of a cleansing process which would allow Earth to absorb outer energies more easily?"

Great assistance is being given right now to all of mankind. Presently, there are twelve of us, twelve Brothers working in this age with Earth itself and also assistants from twelve other solar systems. And while it may seem that this is only happening on this planet Earth, this is happening as well for other planets. This is an ongoing process and a natural one as well. Now for your question, regarding this binding of energy, yes, there has indeed been some of this that has happened but this has only been through the assistance and through those who have asked for it to happen.

Question: "Can you give us the names of the twelve Brothers who are working with Earth now?"

You know the name of six. Six have been revealed, of course myself, El Morya, Kuthumi, Meru, Mafu, and Sananda [the ascended name of Jesus]. Beings from two of the other solar systems have let their presence be known. There are ten more to come.

Question: "Was one known as the Ashtar Command?"

He is one. There was one previous to him and there are ten more to come.

Question: "Is our friend the Grand One one of the Brothers?"

He is a member of the Brotherhood, as we all are, but works on a more intimate level, a level for personal awareness. There are also levels that work for solar awareness. This has been part of the lesson today, understanding solar awareness, how this Earth fits in to a solar system and how our solar system is an integral part of many others. I would like to instruct you on projected awareness.

Saint Germain is taking me now to a kind of a white cube.

Work with a lot of pink light by visualizing yourself sitting on a white cube with pink light bathing all about you and at your feet, a gold light emanating out. Opening up the Third Eye is another important process which must occur here, for to gain inner vision, the inner sight, is an essential part.

24
Finishing Touches and Definitions

Map Refinement

Saint Germain
Kuthumi
El Morya

Since returning to trance work, I've streamlined my technique. First, I've noticed that if I offer my service, a simple statement before entering into the trance state, the channel opens quickly and fluidly. I also start with a personal request: I ask the Spiritual Teacher to, "Show me his light." Saint Germain immediately displays a tube of effulgent white light, and I see well-defined layers of light bodies, with the closest layer next to his ethereal appearance resembling a crackling, violet fire— obviously the Violet Flame that he often speaks of.

Dan has brought a color proof of the I AM America Map for Saint Germain to review in this session. The spiritual teacher runs his finger along the coastline of the Map, which refines and edits its cartography.

With my own new requests and the ones about the Map, this lesson is an exercise in asking for clarity.

❧

We have done a mutual greeting with each other. I'm doing a different process in greeting Saint Germain. Asking to serve as part of the Brotherhood of Light, the Great White Brotherhood, I asked him to show me his light.

I'm glad you're doing this as a precaution, so that the information that you do get is only that of the light. Do you have your questions ready?

Question: "What else did you want us to put on the map before we send it to press? Do you want to show the Heart Chakra or anything else?"

Saint Germain has a pencil out. He's going through the map again, with some corrections that he would like to set in it.

There is a change which will occur in the Salt Lake City area. The coastline will go in a little bit further than indicated on the map there, more toward Wyoming, about fourteen, fourteen in the increments of measurement we were using there. This was an error of interpretation but there are other changes that have occurred since then as well.

In the center of the Heart Chakra, he has placed a dove.

This will be a Center of Peace, universal peace, and this dove will be a symbol for that area. A community will spring up there, though presently, there are very few people inhabiting that area. This center for universal peace will be a place where, not only people from all over our planet will meet, but that this will be an opportunity for people to meet other beings from other solar systems. This Heart Chakra is half way between Malton and Klehma. You have been mispronouncing Malton. It is Mal-tone and also the name of a planet.

Now I would like the other Brothers to take a look at this, Kuthumi and El Morya. They too have been part of this project and bringing it into the physical. This center Heart Chakra will be referred to as the Center of Fire, the Circle of Fire. There is a specific magnetic pull which is there in the center, which is coming into alignment. You can check exactly straight through to the other side of the globe, where the other side falls in Asia. This is a portal which has to do with intergalactic travel. While it is not that necessary that people understand these concepts, it is important that they understand that Earth itself has a Heart Chakra. This is an opportunity for the inhabitants to treat Earth with respect as a living organism. This is not only a Heart Chakra in America but also for Earth.

25

Six principles for walking a path of truth are revealed.

Completion
Saint Germain
Virtue

As we continue with the final edit of the I AM America Map, many more Masters of Light appear and offer their congratulations. No doubt, they are happy that we have returned to our spiritual work and we will soon print the I AM America Map. After several more additions to the Map proof, an ethereal book, "The Book of Truths," manifests and the teachers read from it and give personal advice on the ever-challenging process of spiritual initiation—which we've now entered. I am nervously excited about the publication of the Map. No doubt, once the Map is printed, our lives will never be the same.

There are many in front of me. I am trying to count how many, but Saint Germain is standing with his arm out welcoming me. They're all quite happy. He's got a big smile on his face. I asked him to show me his light and he started laughing at me but he did.

A toast and congratulations on your accomplishment! It is with gratitude that we serve one another, for as much as you have given service to the Brotherhood, we give service to you. This is a jewel within the crown, a jeweled completion, a jewel at the end of a cycle. This map is a way to understand the end of cycles, the end of one cycle as the beginning of another, and the continuing process of change. By learning to accept change and to welcome it, mankind will understand that these are the gifts of enlightenment. Total awareness is expansive awareness. Reaching beyond your present understanding, you are now able to experience a new world beyond the senses. Let me rephrase this. As you walk within your feeling world, you will begin to experience a change within your own feeling world to expand this consciousness.

While at times and presently you feel uncomfortable, welcome this, for this too is a way to expand. With the expansion of the senses, you will be able to expand and shed what is no longer useful. And while this expansion eventually leaves the physical, the emphasis is still on the physical, for within the physical is the building block for the spiritual. The two compliment one another and yet are not of each other. This is a project you've worked on many, many times before but this is the first time it has been brought to completion and as an ongoing process, it will continue, for it too will expand.

Let us continue with the map and the winds moving from the north to the south. The winds are from the shift of the axis. There is a center point for some of these winds, a sort of trail within the southwestern and southern areas. People from South America can come up through these trails to give them an opportunity to experience the expansion which is occurring. There will be a trail that branches off through the state of Colorado.

Question: "Do you want us to show this trail?"

It's not necessary on this map to show it but I wanted to give the information. There's another being here who's looking this over very carefully. He's a being concerned about the Elemental Forces at work and has called for their protection. He is a Master Deva.

I want to stop and rest a while. This is something personal for me. They have done some work on my Third Eye Chakra and they are starting to open up a book, a book called the Book of Truths. This is a process of Initiation. It's brought through the Blue Ray, the All-seeing Eye of God. The first page:

> Welcome to the Path of Truth. From these living waters the thirst is quenched. Beyond the illusion of time is a reality unknown to man, known to God and yet to be revealed. Take this as your guide, for while its passage is personal, its principles are universal in being.
>
> *Number One*: All that is unseen is clearly seen.
>
> *Number Two*: Forget the past, project not to the future, understand time as an illusion and live the moment in its entirety of completion.
>
> *Number Three*: Today is your day as all beings experience it. Walk in union, Brotherhood and peace of your being.

Number Four: Listen with a kind heart. Strive to hear the whisper of God in all you do and see.

Number Five: Walk in the dust and shake it from your feet and give thanks for your obstacles.

Number Six: You are here for yourself and to learn from others. This you will learn for the next sixty days as your Higher Self will draw this and these experiences to you.

Now they are closing and locking this book back up and saying to me: Rest in the peace of God.

It is with great joy from my heart that I commend you and channel the light of truth to your heart. Welcome Brothers, for we are ONE.

A very tall being named Virtue begins to speak about a five Vortex system.

Five vortices have the spinning action that runs in a counter clockwise movement. From this spinning action is a shooting off. The vortices have been created as part of a cleansing process, for they draw up into them energies that spin and shoot out into the universe. They help to consume some of the energies from the center of Earth. At .80 density there will be less changes. As an important part of this cleansing process, they take the toxins out for the expansion of consciousness.

Virtue has left and Saint Germain steps forward. It's taking me a while to make this change. There's a difference in vibratory rate and some interference. This is a personal lesson for me to keep the channel open during a vibrational change. Having the channel open for Saint Germain means it is open to many different things.

I purposely made this three dimensional map so there would be a clearer picture of the exact locations of the coastline. There are some changes which are important: the Heart Chakra, of which you have the change intact; a change at Manitoba which should be documented; easterly winds coming from the northeast through Fargo, North Dakota. A canyon will be formed within that area, west of Fargo.

.

26

*Self-acceptance and expanded spiritual vision
shed light on our fears and human struggles.*

Judgment

I still have some fears associated with printing the Map and how others, outside
of our small circle of supportive friends, may perceive us. In this short lesson, Saint
Germain explains that it is not others' perceptions that we should concern ourselves
with, but rather contemplate how we see ourselves—and the purpose that is
inevitably contained in every little twist and turn of the spiritual path. Acceptance of
self and circumstance, and expanded spiritual vision eliminate the chronic see-saw of
polarized struggle. No doubt, we are our worst critics!

≋

Saint Germain is greeting me and holding up a cross, a flamed cross.

The cross is everlasting light and union. Welcome to the Golden Retreat, a retreat
of son-ship and fellowship.

*In his other hand is sort of a ball of weights and measures. This ball is a very heavy
ball. He is showing this as the contrast between the darkness and the light and how we
constantly work within the movement between these two factors.*

This is what you call "judgment," moving between them. But you do not have to
move between them at all. When you learn the value of acceptance, acceptance of
the weight of the world for what it is and then the acceptance of the light, the light
of son-ship for what it is, then you make the clear choice of where you prefer to be.
This is a power struggle and understanding the will of God. This is a struggle that
occurs naturally within the scope of being human. As you expand your awareness
into the spiritual, you then realize that you can let go of the struggle and see it
clearly for what it is.

You could look at it this way, when you are up in a plane, it is so clear to look down upon what is beneath you. When you are down on the ground and look up at the sky, you may wonder what it would be like to be in the sky. But from the sky, you look down upon Earth and see it for what it is, for you have been there. You could not have gone to the sky without flying from Earth up. It's always easier to see where you've been and the many paths that you have taken. But don't be distraught over paths you have taken, for each path has had its purpose, allowing you to develop the wisdom you need at this moment.

27

It's not the tree—it's the fruit of the tree.

Seeds of the Future

Saint Germain
Euclid

Two new teachers join together for this prophetic lesson on gardening techniques of the future. The metaphor of the ever-bearing spiritual seed is not missed; nothing is wasted on a spiritual journey. So never think you've been there and done that . . . you never know when a new dream, like the ripe, luscious fruit of a tree, may appear.

Saint Germain has taken a pear and sliced it open.

Now we should talk about the fruits of our labors. You take this pear and cut it open and you see the seeds inside, each one ready to be cast upon Earth to shed a new plant and bring a new dream. This is what is meant by the fruits of our labors. Compared again to this tree, you planted the seed and it bore fruit and you eat of the fruit and discard the core, thinking that it is wasted, that it is only garbage. But inside of that core is the seed that plants the new tree, ready to be nurtured. Remember this in times of transition when you've eaten the fruit and you're ready to throw the core, for the fruit will bear again and again and again. Speaking of fruit. . .

Saint Germain is taking us on a tour of a garden, an orchard that is in a kind of a room that has a misting apparatus. The trees don't grow in any type of earth or anything. They are sustained by whatever is in the mist and a sort of matted root system that they all work with. They don't need light and they don't need anything else. The substance is absorbed through the leaves and they are able to continue their process of photosynthesis. This is an actual physical tree that will soon be discovered in science, particularly after the Time of Change. He is also showing me some sort of a tree which looks like a huge tomato tree. When I look at it closely, it looks like a combination of a tomato and a strawberry growing on this large tree.

This process also speeds up the maturation of fruits and vegetables, allowing a complete process in ten to fifteen days for some and twenty to thirty days for others. This is why it is important to save seeds, for seeds will be the one commodity that, while we have the technology, it will be difficult to get the seed to get this started. There's another entity who would be working on this process, Euclid. He is closely tied to the Elementals and would like to be contacted if this is a project you would wish to research and work upon.

Euclid has a different type of look, a kind of a greenish-blue tinge to him, perhaps an Elemental. I'm asking him to show me his light. He is holding up his hands and it is spreading all around in this greenhouse.

This is an application that could be used for any type of seed, although one must be careful in the dosage that is given to each variety and species. We are quite careful with many of the flowers because of the other Elemental Forces. Their full cooperation needs to be given. Lady Mier, another one of the Elementals, works specifically with flower growing and their scents. She is here to assist anyone who would like to work with this as an integral part of vibratory action.

Question: "Where does Euclid come from?"

It is a planet called Carmtax that has an atmosphere of very thick gas. This was a technology that was used there before it came into its last Golden Age. Understand that Earth has not yet entered its Golden Age and this is the transitory period. The Masters will release the technology of the ages to the masses, which will allow many opportunities for spiritual growth and evolution. It is so simple, all one must do is ask.

Question: "What type of a chemical is in this mist?"

A carbon-hybrid. It has copper in it and trace elements of fluoride. It's put through a process with small specks of gold, which causes an interaction. The process of photosynthesis is exactly what it says, photo-synthesis. Break that apart and you will get an idea of how this chemical is put together to interact with organic material.

28

Light bodies move into Oneness.

Kamiak Butte
Madame Blavatsky
Master of Oneness

One Saturday evening, our spiritual group caravanned up to Kamiak Butte for a full-moon meditation. As the sun escaped into the twilight and the moonlight lit our consciousness, the voices of Madame Blavatsky, Master Kuthumi, and the Master of Oneness resounded from the beautiful mountain.

We met last night with a healing group up on Kamiak Butte. We did a meditation in the full moon. During my meditation, Madame Blavatsky came to me for the first time and shared information about the butte. It was once an island and a very ancient piece of land. It is a place to get grounded and feel the energies of the Mother Earth.

Kuthumi presented himself to introduce an entity called the Master of Oneness. I felt a tube of light all around us, projecting up into the sky. The Master of Oneness is closely related to the Elementals and helped align the chakras of our physical body and our light bodies into Oneness. My feeling is that since Kamiak Butte is the Ascension Mountain, a mountain of light, that he will be the Master working there to help the masses with their Ascensions thorough this process of coming into Oneness.

29

The crux of spiritual phenomenon: surrender and acceptance.

Light Travel
Saint Germain
Master of Oneness

A few days ago, I wrote the check to pay for the first press run of the Map. This is, of course, the ultimate leap-of-faith, and deep inside I *know* that everything will be okay. I've decided to leave my sales job; it was only a temporary job anyway and it gave me the needed extra cash flow to help establish our new business: I AM America. That sounds like a big corporation!

Dan and I are getting along perhaps the best we ever have. He hasn't asked the spiritual teachers a question about his finances for almost a month, and although I know the pressure is still silently there, I can tell that he is enjoying the challenge of organizing the I AM America office. He's asked me to move in with him. I really love the little apartment I moved into after I sold my home. Across from it is a terrific park for the kids, and the building is newly renovated, with a Victorian character and hardwood floors. In spite of the gnawing feeling not to do so, I say "yes." This will save money, I tell myself: two can live as cheaply as one. Like Dan, I surrender to the process.

No doubt, my channeling experience of the Master Teachers has deepened significantly. Perhaps this is a mirror of our commitments: Dan's and mine to each other as well as our mutual dedication to the Masters' work with the anticipated publishing of the I AM America Map.

The following is a lesson on achieving Mastery and how our consciousness can travel or project through certain chakras of the human energy system. This whets our paranormal appetite, yet we are astutely reminded by Saint Germain that this phenomenon is grounded in the spiritual tenets of surrender and acceptance. Apparently astral travel is also a natural result of the thinning of the veil between third and fourth dimensional experience.

Saint Germain is welcoming me and handing me a red rose.

The sweetness of success is the sweetness of knowing your being. Let's talk about the vastness of the universe. While at times we think that the universe is filled with nothingness, it is filled with very much. All of the planets are connected through the Web of Time, as you would call it in your dimension. They are really all ONE, so travel between them is possible through this method. This web is in the process of being discovered. It is associated with sound and how sound travels, with light and how light travels, and how energy is transformed and travels.

Saint Germain has a flat table knife in front of me to show me this concept. He is bending the blade and showing that as you bend it, the blade has gone into another area, yet it is still the knife. Then he flattens it back, returning it to its original shape.

This is a concept that could be used for travel among the universe without worrying about what you understand now as light years and the speed of sound. Shedding the present misunderstanding, your energy does not have to be propelled as it is. You can take your energy and adjust it and project it. This is a spiritual process and its meditation starts with the navel. Remember that the focus of energy is at the navel. This is where you have attached, not only to the womb but you have attached your form to materiality. Focus next upon the top of the head where the silver cord is located and then the Third Eye Chakra, through which you travel. Focus on these three energy points. Anchor and ground yourself at the navel. Protect yourself in your travels through the light from the top. And project yourself from your Third Eye Chakra. For exercises before getting ready to travel, focus upon these points and expand the energy belt around them. You are taking your consciousness and your physical matter and learning how to bend it.

Question: "Is this a projection of our consciousness or our astral body, a certain level of our being or all of these?"

My Dear one, it is you, your true essence which will travel. Remember, this is your consciousness, your consciousness that has taken the physical on. It is your consciousness that can do anything with the physical. We are learning Mastery here of the physical and these steps, if taken, can produce fine results, for you are a spiritual entity who has attached to physical matter. And while it feels like you are swimming in a pond of muck, you are still swimming and you have learned to adjust your movement to get to the other side.

This form of travel takes the blood and thins it. It is a thinning of the sheath of the cells of your body and yes, there are finer bodies that exist above the density of the physical. These are the levels of incarnation and embodiment, for as you embodied, you felt the sheath which you broke through. You will learn to use this as a way to travel with a projected conscious feeling, projected conscious touch, smell and, sight.

Question: "Is this similar to what Lori does now as she projects herself into the future to see how things will be?"

It is very similar but she is not yet using her physical matter, as I will instruct you both. For the next three days, practice the visualizations of the three energy points, projecting your energy in a triangular shape for no more than a three-minute period. Practice this first; it is the key to Oneness. While you may adjust energies throughout your system, you still must recognize them as coming from the ONE Source. For in this work, you will be removing the separation which you feel and manifest in all different forms. For when you take three times three times three, what do you get? But when you take one times one times one, what do you get? Mastery is an art. There is nothing that you must overcome. There is nothing that you must work to get. Mastery is letting go and surrendering. The thinning of the Veil will continue.

The Master of Oneness is now entering the teaching. He is showing me his face and I'm trying to see how he appears. He's laughing about my talking about the way he looks. He's balding around the top and his hair comes down to his shoulders. It is grey, his eyes are blue, his robe has the symbol of a gold circle, signifying the Master of Oneness.

Surrender is acceptance. You don't know, you can't do it, and the piece to the puzzle isn't there, and yet by your surrender, of acceptance of that, you gain it. This goes beyond trying. This goes beyond doing. This walks into the realm of being who you are. And yes, this is general information but remember the strength of my being and that each time you surrender that bit of you and take the lead weights off of your arms, your legs, your eyes and thin the Veil, remember I AM here, all in Oneness.

Light = sound

30

*First, feel the Oneness—this introduces
the basics of light and sound.*

Light and Sound

We are light, and we are sound. These are two of the esoteric laws of creation. In this introductory lesson, Saint Germain introduces the metaphysical underpinning of the ONE. However, in order to visualize the resonance of light and sound, we must learn to feel Oneness. Don't forget, in the beginning we are all the same light—and this pattern of light is the same in the aura of the human and the aura of Earth.

Saint Germain is giving me a sort of party of lights. It's beautiful. Now he's ready to talk.

Exploring the building blocks of the universe begins with light and vibration. Light equals sound. It's upon the portal, the inverted V coming down from the light that equals sound to resonance and then another V on the top of this is the life force. The circle all around these is universal principles, the inner to the outer, the microcosm to the macrocosm, the inner core to the outer core. Within your own vibratory rate is light and sound.

The way you recognize the different principles of light and sound is how light and sound take on the different resonance to produce a different quality of life. This is an energetic molecular structure that is present in all things, even at the ascended level, for again, it is a continuing process. Do not believe for an instant that you shed light for sound, for it too goes on and takes on a higher finer quality in Ascension. In the Bible, it is said that in the beginning there is light. There always is the light. Remember, it is the foundation and the universal building block. Not only do we have molecular structure at the physical level, but molecular structure of the spiritual realms. Visualize this molecular structure at all times within your being, for it is your true composition.

Take five like bubbles and it comprises the cellular being, representative of the physical level in light and sound. While you don't understand this in the present moment, your sense of touch is relative to light and sound. Your sense of taste is relative to light and sound. Of course your vision is light and sound and so is your audible hearing system. Realize as you develop the higher awareness, the higher sense, it is not a shedding of sensation but the expansion of the same and the awareness that these are the principles from which your sensation comes from.

Upon these five cellular groupings is a growth process, having more circles and more circles of completion. Within the inner core, the middle bubble, is a direct link to the .124 revolutions per millisecond and the Divine Source. This fine thread, this silver cord, runs through the center of all of these. Now, the triangular shape inside is turning and pivoting around this cord inside, running through the center, and more of the circles are stacked on top. Underneath these are principles for precipitation, for this is the structure of universal substance. You are a form, a crystalline substance, a condensation of vibratory rate of light and sound, all at their intersections. The action and the spinning and blending determine density.

You must have a belief in these principles, command them to your use, for remember in the beginning there was light. Now, for instance, in the precipitation of gold, you have a lower tuned vibration compared to the human energetic body. And yet, in the Mineral Kingdom, it is the highest vibration of substances classified in First Density. Next is the crystalline and gem structures. Next to that is lapis, the blue stone. If you were to study the universal of these, you would find within it the same principles I have described to you here, for the structure is the common denominator among all things. This is the principle that you must learn and learn to command.

Response: "I remember reading about this in *Life and Teachings of the Masters of the Far East*, where one of the Masters precipitated by visualizing a molecule or atom and building up around it."

Remember the number ten and that it is in the rotating. It is no mistake that your Earth is a round sphere with two poles, for this has been a replica of the Divine Structure within the universe. Visualizing the rotating creates the magnetism to draw more to it, to grow into the physical form. The rotating determines the form. We are talking about the principles of light and sound and allowing light and sound to enter into the existing structure. The molecular structure is similar to Earth, similar to all planets, for this is the perfection and the symbol of the universal structure and the resonance of light and sound. The floor is open for questions.

Question: "Since we don't know the particular resonance of the different materials, we would just visualize that particular material and the consciousness would center the molecule, then connect with that resonance?"

You must learn to feel resonance, you must learn to take your own resonance and sense within it what it is. To feel the Oneness, realize that you comprise the same substance as everyone and everything. In your understanding of your sameness and your Oneness, you command. To put it on a level of understanding with the mental faculties, visualize the first molecule, then add more gathering around the molecule, in light and sound. Start with the principle of building five together. With gold there are two from which you build, but human form has five from which it builds. But remember, it is all the same. In the beginning there is light.

Question: "So with gold, is that the two bubbles you are referring to?"

Yes, the two bubbles. But then gold is the highest physical Vibration of Light and you can hear within it a sound. In fact, very often sound is mistaken for the sense of taste within the human system. Small children, when they first come into embodiment, what do they do, they hear the objects, they put them in their mouth. Remember, when we speak in these sessions, we speak with a structured simplistic form and there is much more detail for you to discover. These are the building blocks to open the doors, the opportunity for you to learn and discover.

Within the Chakra System is this structure again. You have the five building blocks, the five circles, the five spheres on each of your chakra points at the eighth energetic body and what is it that runs through at the top. The silver cord. Now do you see this principle at work?

Response: "So the cord goes through these spheres from point to point."

That is correct, gathering and gathering and gathering. And in the attraction of people and souls to one another, this same principle is at work. The gathering of ONE to Itself is the expanding consciousness. This is exactly the principle of which I'm speaking. While we see the expansion, we also see the centering of the ONE. This is the purpose for the message of Oneness and the work which we have been doing. It will be a principle you will see over and over and over as you are being given the proof and yet, this session is the proof. The stacking crosses currents. We have crossed currents and these comprise levels of consciousness which you will term the physical, the astral planes of the psychic realm, the spiritual planes of the soul, and the planes beyond, from which we function. Again, they are all ONE, the continuum of life. Look at Earth itself, she has the most simplistic structure. Does she not have atmospheric layers? And drawn to her are the other planets. As she is drawn to them, they are drawn to her. Now I return the floor with your permission. I AM Saint Germain.

31

The power of the Source is the circle of life.

The Storehouse

One of the purposes of the Brotherhood of Spiritual Teachers is to free mankind physically through the knowledge of science, and spiritually by fostering our inner growth and evolution. This lesson addresses the unique power that is hidden in the omnipresent Source which is the basis of all technological advancement. Saint Germain escorts us to an ethereal storehouse where he reveals new technology for the future.

✍

We walk into a room and there's a lot of green light all around in the room and Saint Germain is welcoming me to what he calls the storehouse of surprises. In this room are many of the surprises and inventions which the Brotherhood is ready to release for the benefit of mankind.

We have said over and over, all you must do is ask.

And they are here. Now, in front of me is a box. He's laughing as he is showing this to me. It's a microwave oven.

This has taken the element of time and used it upon a wavelength and yet, how many more grand projects and products are available to benefit mankind. And where is the source of all this? The Source is here. The Source is knowing that you are ONE and realizing the energy from the Source in a true productive manner. It is through the great love the Brotherhood has for mankind, understanding the struggle of the physical as we had to. Dear ones, we see your struggle and understand the temptations, for this is Mastery and in the fullness, we realize power and come to understand the highest Source.

In front of me is a ball, sort of cloudy inside.

Put your hands on it. It gives you a total physiological adjustment of all the Chakra Systems. While the power may appear to be for the physical, as the dense layers on the physical body benefit from the use of this, it is also through your conscious awareness, the source of where this comes from, that you experience a more everlasting and invigorating affect for your mind, body, and spirit. We are concerned with freeing mankind and while mankind struggles with physical need, we shall endeavor to lift the shackle. If we must do it through these products, then it is so. And yet, we shall also endeavor to bring the highest awareness at all times, even from the simple microwave to that which is in store. You may exclaim and say what a contrast but there really is none, for it's all from the same Source and the same means to the end. And yet, the end is only a beginning. For again, the path is a path of a spiral and contained within this path is the Divine Circle of Completion. For the spiral runs not as a triangular or square shape but a circular motion, not an angular motion. This is a mathematical principle of all that is life. Through the spiral, we bore the holes into the unknown and find what has been known for ages.

Several are standing around with their hands on this object, clearing their etheric bodies which filters into the physical.

Placing not only an electrical charge but a magnetic force field bonds energies into a synthesis for one process. Disease of the physical is that dis-ease. It's a scattering of energy away from the function of its true form. And yet disease has also happened to the spiritual bodies. The energy has been scattered away from its true form. Through your exercises, you are learning to refocus your energies, to bring them and gather them and use them for the true function of the form. Energies which you may have projected upon other entities will now be gathered. Energies that you have projected into your own being will be gathered up. This use and this application of these energies can now be transformed and reused and refocused. You thought this was energy which had been dissipated but there is no such thing. All that you do and all that you have done can be gathered unto you and used as tools for awakening, not only your physical but your finer bodies.

Now we walk on to a huge triangle that you can stand in.

Bathing is a process for cleansing the physical body and yet, if mankind would understand how refreshed they feel after this process, they would realize that bathing is the intermingling of Elemental Life Force into the finer body that produces this state of cleanliness. Cleansing of the spiritual results in the physical.

Now he's showing me this triangular-shaped object. It's high enough for you to stand in, sort of a waterless shower with a base and two sides.

This too comes from the Source and draws its symbology from the trinity. The triangle is man's union and dominion over matter, which is how we are truly cleansed. Are there any questions?

Question: "Should we be gathering the information about the products and putting it out in a newsletter, so that whoever has the capabilities and incentive to work on these will have this information?"

If you wish, but the Masters know who will do this work. We will continue to send the information, for there is no mystery to the things which God does.

Question: "Is there a power source to it?"

It has a certain structure to the inner core. It may be accomplished through the use of electricity and yet can be and will be simplified to use power from another source. The energy source is of major importance. The etheric rehabilitator is second. Through the knowledge of these two, you will construct the third, for this is the way that this process will work. As this technology is ushered through, it will open the door for even more. We will work to perfect your first project which has been your training ground. While it may appear to be a simple device and have such limited impact upon mankind, you will be sweetly surprised. Proceed with the love and the blessings of the Brotherhood.

32

*The Christ Consciousness is the basis of universal
friendship, love, brotherhood, and Oneness.*

Brotherhood

We have had some intense pressures: organizing the office, moving, and the Maps—the I AM America Maps have shipped! Interestingly, it is often not in peace but in strained and pressured situations that we need spiritual guidance the most, and this is perhaps one of the most insight-packed channelings we've received to date. Two Spiritual Teachers, Saint Germain and Sananda, share their insights on what is truth and how to respect and honor the spiritual truths of others. According to their teachings, this is the heart of understanding the Christ within, as universal friendship, love, and brotherhood.

You are right to refer to us as your Brothers, to not place us in the position of celebration or worship. It was not the original intent that we be placed in a position of control over you but rather in a position of Brotherhood, where we can extend our hand in service. It is in service to humanity that we come and you too must recognize this relationship to work with us. It is with great humility and gratitude that we perform the service and when you come to ask, ask as you would ask a friend instead of as a favor from a king. This is not a favor that we do for you. This is the gratitude of our service. It is a combination of work upon the Seven Rays, primarily the Love Ray which is the Pink Ray, that which we need to flood the Earth with at this present moment. The truth of your being has realized the true inner working of the Violet Ray, for the truth of the ages has been adulterated. But only through the human has this been able to occur. Beloved Sananda has said, I AM the way, I AM the truth, and what was this service upon? The Blue Ray. For it is the I AM activity that we are extending to all our Brothers upon the face of this planet and the focus of the Pink Ray is what is needed most at this Time of Transition.

This love is unconditional. When it is conditional, look within the spectrum and pull from it that which is the true quality of love. Look within the love itself and find the quality of truth, for is not truthful love the cleansing and the purging? Is not this form of love transformation and transforming? And as you are transformed from a cocoon to a butterfly, is not this the Violet Ray? With forgiveness of yourself, you extend forgiveness to others. Now I would like to turn the floor over to Sananda.

It was true that my work done in the Piscean Age was that of showing the way, the path of unconditional love, the extended hand of forgiveness, forgiving as you would also like to be forgiven. Now, as we merge into the New Times, we will explore in the next twenty years, the dissemination and knowledge of all that is love. And is not all but just what is love combined with truth, truth as you realize it, truth as others realize it, acknowledgement that all have their own sense of truth? And in Brotherhood, are we not all seeking but this, the truth? Allow your Brother then to find his own truth, as you have found yours. Do not place the condition where there is control that his truth must be your truth, for in the inner most part of your being, you know that truth which is for you and in the inner most part of his being, he stands firm within his truth. And as you would like to be respected for the knowledge of your truths, he too must be respected for the knowledge of his. And is this but the Violet Ray? Is this but the New Age? Is this but all ONE? And while we all express the one truth, the one love, the one transformation, it is truly individualized, but individualized for each one.

Saint Germain has given you three plus three equals ONE, for as your Brother stands for truth and love and transformation and as you stand for truth and love and transformation, he and the three, you and the three, don't you but stand for the ONE as you would say, the means to the ends? But try, continue to try. There are times when you would like to give up. Remember this, your Brother is no different than you and you're no different than your Brother. And remember this too, when you look to the Brothers of the Brotherhood, they are no different from you, you're no different from them. We are not kings, we are your friends, we are your helpers. What is but a king? A person put into control for a period of time. But what is a Brother? A Brother is a continuing process, everlasting. Can you say this person is my king? No, but you can say this person is my friend. Yes, and is this not timeless? For this is the age that is upon you.

Recognize the Christ within all, the Christ that is truly that which is seeking the truth as they come to see it. What is the Christ but love and love is the universal principle and recognizing that each has their own truth? And what does this do when we give this unconditional recognition? We are transformed, we are extended, we are carried to a level of understanding, a level of existence that transforms our beings, our thoughts, our wishes, our hearts, our desires, and yes, even the physical body. Understand this true principle, the principle of Oneness.

Saint Germain is coming back into the room.

We had discussed these same principles before. I have shown you them structurally within the pyramid. The four points which you guide to the one at the top, the unity of man over materiality, the points being the soul, spirit, body, mind. Ask that support is there for you at all times. If you feel like a fish out of water, your gills extended, what is the thing to do but to jump back into the water. And yet once you've been through the experience, you swim differently. Do you feel like you are swimming differently?

Response: "Well, it takes me a lot less time to get my head turned around when I start feeling pressure."

This is the work you choose to do?

Response: "Of course."

When you feel tired, mentally strained, you must seek your time alone and realize the source of your being and call, ask us, your friends. You are concerned about being open. Do not bother yourself with that. We will assist you. You are trying to do this yourself and no man does it himself. Do as you are doing. Apply yourself in most constructed effort. Let your friends be of assistance to you, for this is our work as well as yours. As long as you have the willing desire. That is all that is needed. When you are tired, put yourself anyplace where you may ask and say "I have the willing desire, please assist me at this moment" and then accept the assistance as you would accept a basket of bread from your best friend. Then remember, I AM here.

And now before we start this discourse, close your eyes and feel this energy and remember I AM a being of Violet Fire, for is not the Violet Flame the continued desire for the evolution of the consciousness of mankind? I AM the purity that God desires. Now, do your work, as you are sealed in the Violet Flame and sealed with the essence of the white light. Do your work and keep your focus. There are many, many that are doing the same. Your friends are here and do not be worried over the foolishness of your openness, for it is your desire and continue to ask, for how could you not be loved? Would God open one of his flowers and not the others? For you are the same creation as all others. You are the same flower and yet your scent and your color may be different. You have a right to be here like all the others. And the rain falls upon you as it falls upon the others and the earth is the same from which you grow as the others grow too. Remember, we are truly your friends, united in Brotherhood, truth, love, and transformation.

33

Nothing is as simple as it may seem!

Simplicity

Kuthumi

When it is appropriate, the Spiritual Teachers will reveal past lives, and especially incidents from certain lifetimes that still hold important spiritual lessons relevant to our present state of spiritual growth. The Spiritual Teacher Kuthumi explains that some lifetimes are inordinately simple, while others are more complex. Recognition of this spiritual truth is also an important lesson about standing back to gain perspective and spiritual insight without judging another. Most importantly, we are reminded to never forget that every life, from the unpretentious to the most intricate, is part of the whole.

I must admit that this is difficult, especially since we've had some flack from naysayers about the Map and our beliefs that surround its teachings. Fortunately Dan came right out and asked the Spiritual Teachers for advice about this. Their counsel in a nutshell: "this information is not for everyone." They recap this lesson with a profound statement on change. I won't paraphrase here, so read the entire paragraph. It begins with the words, "We cannot stop something, but we can change the course . . ."

I sat down to rest and Kuthumi handed me a little brown rabbit. I was thinking about some things he had shown me relating to a spaceship from our past history and was feeling there was still more to be revealed about that time. Now he is showing me an embodiment where I knew him as Saint Francis. I have a cart that I am pushing and loading rock and dirt into it. I am working at this church or monastery and building something. I hurt my shoulder, a deep cut. He came over and touched it, took care of it. I am happy.

Dear one, unconditional healing is being able to give that out of yourself, for you do not know where that person may be, who that person really truly is. In that embodiment, you expressed simplicity and yet your whole collective consciousness was not that simple. That was a lifetime, a fragmented lifetime of expressing one thing. There are times, lifetimes, where one petal must be formed until you have the opportunity to come to full bloom in an embodiment. This is before one flowers, as you have in this opportunity, this time to be the full flower. As you go, you shall encounter many who also are in full bloom and many who express just the fragments. Understand this and still give unconditionally, for they are still part of the whole and must be nurtured to grow.

As I hand you this rabbit and you feel the brown fur, it is only a fragment of the Animal Kingdom. And yet does it not, so simply express the loving and simple honesty of this Kingdom of the Animals. So, as I show this to you and you pet it and you hold it, this fragment of the collective consciousness, it is still part of the whole. Does it not deserve recognition from yourself of that which it is? It is peace. See this and look for this in others. As you see this in this rabbit, do you not see this in others, for they are presently simple expressions and this expression is part of their path, their plan? Stand back away from judgment. Their development is where it is. Their development is, as you say, par for the course. Where do you think this saying came from, par for the course? Remember this simple honest embodiment which you had. You chose that path. The simple honest rabbit that you hold, you choose to see the fragment. The Animal and the Mineral Kingdom for which I work to cleanse will only come to completion through the application of universal principle.

Question: "I have been criticized a couple times for the information on the map by people questioning its validity. What is a good way to handle this?"

We have given the map with a directive purpose, for this is what the Masters know and serve and no one should question what purpose it serves for each person. When you are criticized, turn your back on this judgment and do not judge them, for you do not know the purpose this information has for them. Perhaps for them, it is to turn their back upon. Then it is so. Perhaps it is for them to take up and to plant the seed within. This is what its purpose is for. Again, some express the fragments and some express the collection of many and would this not best appeal to those of the collective. You will also encounter the fragments. Accept them through the simple joy of knowing that they too have Divine Purpose.

Question: "There are many who still believe that if there are enough lightworkers that open up that these changes will not have to happen. Then, if this is the case and it doesn't come to pass, then the map will have served its purpose?"

We cannot stop something, but we can change the course. You are traveling down the river and you are in the water. You can swim, you can paddle, you can float, you can travel down one side of the bank and yet you are having difficulty getting out, for the current is swift. But what do you do, reach out and get out of the water and watch the river roll by? And if you do, you are still wet, for you have been in the river. Do this with great care and understanding, for you are all in the river together. It is in love for mankind that we have sent this work. Acceptance is the key to harmony in this work.

34

*Even when the circumstances are undeniably
physical, the solution is still spiritual.*

Time Equals Love
Saint Germain

For more than a month I've had the date October 17 engrained in my mind. I asked for guidance but did not receive any more information. In fact, I asked an acquaintance, also a seasoned channeler, in session with her Spirit Guide if October 17 could be the date for a major Earth Change event? His response: "Each day is a turning point, as a day to present something new to the world."

Well, his counsel was spot on and so was my intuition. On October 17 at 5:04 p.m. a 6.9 earthquake struck the San Francisco Bay area. The earthquake caused severe damage and many buildings collapsed.

I can't help but think of the Maps—now in transit to our office—and how important the message of the Spiritual Teachers may be in ameliorating future events such as these. In the following lesson, we asked about future earthquakes and the answer is surprising. Each earth movement, big or small, is all about Earth's shift into higher consciousness. And as disastrous as the Great Purification of Earth may seem, Sananda's ever-present guidance is, "All is love."

No doubt, as soon as the Maps arrive, we'll have a lot of work ahead of us. The Spiritual Teachers must know this too, and end this teaching with a decree for protection and spiritual awakening from Archangel Michael.

Question: "What more can you share about the earthquakes on the West coast and also on the other side of the planet?"

We have talked about thermodynamics. Now this is the Law of Motion, $E=mc^2$, [energy equals mass times the velocity of light square], precisely the formula that works. You are very aware of this, for the plates on the ocean floor have shifted. The cosmic force from the center of Earth is being released. As you call for the purifying of your vessels through the Violet Flame, call for the purifying of the Earth vessel through the Gold Flame. The Divine silver cord, running within the inner core, magnetically pulls layer upon layer upon layer onto this cord. As it shifts to move, the brilliance will be released. The Angelic Host, angels of compassion, Archangel Michael, have truly sent their radiance and they are here at your command. For as you know, the lightworkers, the light bearers, are ready to take their stand. Archangel Michael has chosen to be the one of the Blue Flame of protection, protection of the innocence of God. Do you have any questions?

Question: "Will we be able to know of other events like this beforehand?"

We send the hints, we send the clues, we send the feelings; are these not what the initiate feels, the intuitiveness of an event about to occur, or have you not felt this? As with other events, it is a natural occurrence for those making the call to the inner core of Earth for the purification of the mantle. This needs to be a complete cleansing of the Heart Chakra in all mankind. You think "all is love" is simple and in its beauty it is but it is the application of "all is love" that is so hard for mankind to discover and bring to manifestation. Beloved Sananda has worked to bring this knowledge to you. "All is love" is questioned and not applied, so the lightworkers bring truth to the actions of love. They bring the Blue Ray, the will of God, the Truth Ray to the action of the Pink Ray, love. For is this not the Violet Flame of which we have spoken and continue to pour forth to humanity. I AM THAT I AM is a powerful statement, sealing and directing these energies of light force. I AM THAT I AM is your call to manifest the sealing of the Violet Ray. I AM THAT I AM is the power of God, directed will, directed love, and brought forth in Brotherhood. Use it daily. Use it and apply it.

Just as there are guardian angels, as you will call them, as guides, many of those taken in the quake have been released to work as guides for many of those in physical embodiment. For this too was the work they chose, to come into physical-ness, to progress, and to know the inner core. Yes, it is shocking to be removed violently from the Earth Plane and yet this was the path they chose. So many of the Dear ones will continue their work, continue their work guiding and directing the forces upon the etheric levels of which you are not consciously aware of during waking hours. There are forces which are at work at all times and the time is at hand in what you would call your dimension. For seek ye not the Kingdom of Man, seek ye the Kingdom of God. Is this not the teachings of the Piscean dispensation?

Question: "Does this have to do with the triangular Vortex shapes?"

We have talked much about this inner core and a mathematical wave line as some call it. And yet, it is dimensional mathematics of which we speak, for $E=mc^2$ is only the beginning. The rotational pull of the apex can be explored. When you take an umbrella and it inverts in the wind, the setting up of the core was built upon this Divine shape. Divinity, Divinity is the sound principle of all that is love and yet built upon the Kingdom of God and the Kingdom unfolding. And so as the umbrella unfolds, the energy, where does it go? To the outer. Subtle as the force may seem, it is a powerful one, one which is extending and no force can stop it.

We have talked much about dimensional mathematics, gravitational pull, thermodynamics, theories of relativity, energy, time, and space and yet in the simplest application, you could apply this to time equals love. This is the most simplistic way to understand the cleansing of the Heart Chakra. The solidifying of fact is that which man can only grasp at this moment. It is the same as density of the physical and yet the essence, the Spirit leaves the physical. What happens to the body? Disintegration, absolute disintegration of matter as you have known. And yet where does disintegration go? It continues on in the process of balance and harmony.

Understand solidification, the turning to the dimension of spirit, soul, mathematically, or as you call it, dimensionally, and it's adherence to spiritual and yet physical properties. These are the wonders and mysteries for you, whose consciousness is embedded in the physical. And yet, you will understand this in its most simple, rudimentary form. Time equals love. We will walk you through this formulation, for we understand that with your mind and its capacity, this is your function.

We call to Archangel Michael and ask you to make this call too for this work of protection. The sword of truth and the will of God is that which spins within the microcosm of your being into the macrocosm. Call daily for his use and application. Call for his protection. Call for his sword of awakening. Like the violet lightning in the skies, Archangel Michael is the protector of the will of God, the truth of God, that which ushers in the age of loving Brotherhood. Call for his protection for yourself and for your Brothers of the light. Upon other grounds of your being occurs the pull at all times of the other force of which you are not consciously aware and yet submit yourself to. Call for the direction, for the force of Archangel Michael in your life. Erase fear to the knowingness of love and the truth of that love, the application of that love.

I AM a being of Violet Fire. I AM the purity God desires.
I AM the will of God. I AM the mercy of God.
I AM the protection of God. I AM the all-seeing eye of God.
I AM THAT I AM.
I AM THAT I AM.
I AM THAT I AM.

Dear ones use this in your applications.

35

The real work begins.

Pillars of Service
El Morya
Kuthumi
Sananda
Saint Germain
Serapis Bey

It is October 22 and a large pallet of beautiful I AM America Maps has arrived from our printer in Boise! Our office is organized like expectant parents awaiting the arrival of a newborn—packing material and single white mailing tubes are neatly organized in a wrap-and-pack area. We chose a durable cardboard-like stock for the first press run of the Maps, and we take one home and lay it on the living room floor, inspecting every color and word, now printed in indelible ink.

Dan encourages a trance session, and the Spiritual Teachers seem almost excited as we are. The following lesson is their congratulations and counsel for what I now know was a significant life-changing event. This spiritual advice is written on an ethereal scroll—much like the I AM America Map. However, this scroll is known by our spiritual mentors as the "Truths of Ages." These are four spiritual tenets for achieving and realizing the Christ Consciousness.

✎

Four Ascended Masters are examining the map. Sananda is in the northwest corner. El Morya is standing at the southwest corner. Kuthumi is at the northeast and Saint Germain is at the southeast corner. They are projecting their energies, left hand over the heart, right hand towards the center of the map. Each one of the Masters will be working in the regions closest to where they are standing. Saint Germain will be working in the south for freedom. Kuthumi will be working in the areas of ice, very closely with the Elementals and Devas. Sananda will be working in the northwest for healing. El Morya will be working in the southwestern areas to bring forth the strong, directive force of the Ray of Divine Wisdom, the consistencies of the truth in all works. He would like to speak.

I would like to talk about the inconsistencies of works. We must understand the Will of God, for the Will of God is the one consistent truth. This is the clue or key contained in any material. It must speak of the human will and the intervention of that which is the God Source. We cannot take the time to deal with colorful personalities; you can, for the personalities bring much joy along the path. We need to talk about the consistencies in all material brought in at this time, which turns the conscious will over to the Christ Itself to bring the intuitive knowledge back to Selfhood. We talk about the self and we talk about Selfhood. The self, the smaller self being the little "I," and Selfhood being that ONE taking command, the ONE who has recognized his place in the universal stream. Within this stream is all the knowledge of all that ever was and all that ever will be.

He is unrolling a scroll. Written on the scroll is Truths of Ages. On this scroll is:

Number One: Thou Shalt Have No Other Gods Before Me.

This is the principal of which I speak, of self to Selfhood. We are not here to work with whims or to bend with the winds. We are here to stand for that which is the work of Universal Truth. Everyday, as chelas of this order, you must take the firm stand that this day is yours to responsibly command, but this day does not belong to you. This day belongs to a force which will guide and direct you and this force is anchored deep within you, anchored within the Heart Chakra, as the inverted pyramid of which was spoken to you in similar discourses.

Number Two: Judge Not, Least You Be Judged Yourself.

There is much discussion about judgment versus discernment. Be careful with the thoughts you have, for they can surely manifest. Is not the person who dwells upon the Will of God directed in thought as this Being? Beloved Kuthumi would like to speak on this principal.

Dear ones, dwell upon that which is love for your fellow Brother. Dwell upon that which is what you have surely seen within yourself. When you look upon another and see them doing something which you instinctively know is the wrong action, your first inclination is to point it out. But remember the teachings. Remember that you too have participated long in this experiment. You too have taken many courses of action, for have we not presented action versus reaction? This is the principal of judging. There are many experiences in the physical and it seems so slow and dense and yet the most uplifting of these is to take yourself and stand aside and observe. This is discernment. Take yourself from the present moment and stand aside and look and say I will not judge this, I will observe and learn. Stand aside Dear ones, take time to stand aside. And now Beloved Saint Germain will speak.

And I would like to talk about the Flame of Freedom, the flame which has leaped from the Heart of God, the flame of all men who remember the freedom to express, the freedom to find one's way, the true freedom to be allowed an individual path. For again, you know so well that we are all truly individualized but yet, are we all not of the same Source? This is the same principal. This leads us to. . .

Number Three: Thou Shall Not Covet.

When you covet, are you not infringing upon the freedom of another individual? Your path is separate and unique to you and with Divine Purpose. Give freedom to your Brother, such as you have been given freedom by your great God Self and your great God Source. Do not look upon your Brothers and say "This is the way you should live," as you would not want another to infringe upon your path. This is the true meaning of coveting. Do you not know that you can walk your path with God, hand in hand? Yes, while there are those who will closely believe your truths, as God has planted this flame in your heart, remember you never walk this path alone. Yet, you come to it by allowing others to walk theirs. Sananda will address the fourth principle.

Number Four: Love One Another.

For what is this mission but acceptance. Acceptance is the fourth. Give to one another. Give to each other as you have received. Love one another without conditions, for when you love with expectation, you limit the vibration of this force. See in your Brother that which you too have seen in yourself, as Brother Kuthumi has spoken. Love one another, for it is the highest principal of all.

They are all reciting together:

These are the Pillars on which we stand, the four united to the ONE. And in the center of the apex is the true realization of the Christ Consciousness, the true focus for which man can spiral and use above for the first manifestation as an Initiate.

In the center of this is Master Serapis Bey.

These are the principals of which we prepare to raise the physical to the level of Ascension, which specifically in matter can be directed over time. For as you see, it is your thoughts and your actions which keep you bound.

Saint Germain is taking the floor.

When presented with a Map of Changes, one may encounter great fear and mistrust, doubt, and suspicion as to the source and to the phenomenon. And yet this is not so, as one is faced with only that course of action within one's own being. As the changes occur, we will be here for your assistance, serving as Pillars, for throughout these teachings, we take away the mystery. We take away the secrets, for these have long been hidden, except for those who specifically sought them. Now this information is to be public knowledge, for the upliftment of humanity. For America is a free country and freer than you can presently understand. It is Her, the first embodiment of the Root Race.

Now we come to the end of the cycle of the Seventh Race, completing like clockwork that which has been ordained and set forth. And these many mysteries are not mysteries. They are still simple and true principles given to live your life. These principles exist as these Pillars and we assure you, we are here for your assistance. Ask Beloved ones, ask. I AM at your call night and day.

They bow, and in the center where they projected their hands is a star, a five-pointed star. The points are glowing and in the center is written: The Light Of God Never Fails.

36

*As you begin your spiritual journey never forget
the Godself—the Source.*

Feast of Light

Saint Germain
Dionysus
Sananda
El Morya
Kuthumi
Master of Oneness

We have organized a six-week tour of the West Coast to launch the publication of the Map. My little Pontiac Grand Am is packed to the brim, with more than 500 Maps in the backseat, suitcases, clothes on hangers, alongside a slide presentation that illustrates all of the spiritual information and its accompanying prophecies. Last weekend we presented the material for the first time together at the Gardenia Center in Sandpoint—and it was successful with about 100 people attending. I had no idea that there would be so many people interested in this information!

Dan has organized a list of stops on our way to Los Angeles, and we have several presentations: Boise; Bend and Klamath Falls, Oregon; and a few small towns on the way to Mount Shasta. Last May we sent out a small black-and-white version of the Map and a description of its information to over 1,000 spiritual and metaphysical centers; the response was good. Many of these stops are with spiritual and metaphysical organizations much like our hometown spiritual group. Our budget is tight; no doubt we'll be sleeping on a few living-room couches along the way. Yet overall, it is almost like a door has literally opened to a pathway clearly lit to every individual who wants to know about the I AM America Map.

Last week I made a quick trip to see my children and parents before I left. My mother pled with me, "Oh, please don't do this!" I sensed her protection and an unnerving fear in her words. I asked why. Her response was quick: "This may expose your life to the public . . ." I assured her I would be okay and would be home two weeks before Christmas.

We have another presentation, this time in Boise. Before we leave on this short trip, we ask for guidance and the Spiritual Teachers fortify us with their support and love.

~

We are wearing our seamless white robes. I am standing to the side and you are standing in the center. To the right is Saint Germain. We're holding the map on a gold plate. We're giving it to a council. To the back of the council are four pillars. There is a pillar to the right, one to the left, and two in the back. There are five beings on this council. They are sitting at a round table. The facilitator of this council is Dionysus. Sananda is to the side with Kuthumi and El Morya. Dionysus works on this Council of Justice. It's a court for planetary justice and a review board. Saint Germain is introducing us.

Welcome to the Inner Court of Harmony, the inner court which brings planetary justice to review the work you two have completed and brought forth to the physical for the completion of the cycle. We will review this work for those in the physical. You are just beginning and have seeded this work, for scattered among the planet are many you will work with now, to bring together this fold. It is our wish and our intention to keep this work in the purest light, purest intention, and purest harmony. That they be directed not through fear or discord or through capital gain but that they be directed through the inner desire of the Flame of God which burns within their heart for the cleansing and purification of the Mother Planet. This work will be viewed by some as the work of tribulation and a Time of Tribulation and yet this work is like the gold plate. It is a golden door to open their minds and their hearts to the essence and radiance of the Brotherhood.

Dionysus is speaking.

Beloveds, greetings from my heart, and the Love of God that Never Fails. It is with great joy that we receive this work and we send our vibration, our steadfastness, for it is through the unity of two Brothers working together, united in one focus, which is the example of the productivity of this work. Continue your work in this same light to increase its radiance among the fold and dispense them on this tribunal of council. We shall review and send our radiance to those embodied upon the planet to spark the memory within them to rekindle the message which is planted deep within their heart, the work they have been prepared to do. Discern in your speaking engagements and discern sharing the information, for many will come, many will be interested, and yet, few will truly follow. And we send our radiance, these Pillars to light this work.

And now we ask you to drink from the Cup with us for the completion of the seeding. I raise my glass, this Cup, with Divine Joy for the quality of the work completed. And as you travel and sup and drink with others, remember this feast with the council and the direction of your work. Do not forget the Source from which it came and which it is now returning to. For again, as this work has gone full circle among the planet, it returns back to its Source and again is dispensed in its pure, lighter form. For this is the true work of the lightworker, to refine the highest message and the highest truth. This is our toast.

A great being of light enters, the Master of Oneness. He speaks.

The work of the Fire Ascension is that of the unity of force. Brother to Brother, unity of force, united in truth, acceptance of truth without judgment is the eternal Wisdom of the Ages. For the next step of this project is the uniting of those within the physical embodiment. The preparation of the physical, the preparation of the body, the purification of the body is much like the purification of the Earth and Earth ascending. Becoming ready to ascend, such is the body of the lightworker being prepared.

As you remember in the temples, we worked with the anointment of the herbs and the oils. We spread the oils upon your body and your finer bodies. We are ready to smooth the jagged lines, such as oil will smooth the jagged lines on your physical bodies. We work to smooth the jagged lines of your inner being and your outer light shell, which you are ready to expand your being into. Such as the body is prepared and purified, we too will work for the purification of the outer body from which the inner may radiate out to. Understand Dear ones, this is a process which you perceive as taking time and yet we perceive, not as that in time but that which is made ready. Complete your work with joy and do not forget the Source. Amen! Amen! Amen!

He's sitting down. Sananda is standing up to speak.

You might refer to this as a similar scene from what was called the Last Supper but we call this a Feast of Light, the first of many. And as we gather you up into the fold, behold the true feast, the light of your being. Do this in remembrance of the Source.

He's sitting down. El Morya is rising.

True wisdom is that which not only comes from the heart. True wisdom is that which recognizes the Source at all times. Recognize this Source, the Godself, as the Universal Presence, that which holds all together.

Kuthumi now speaks.

  Be gentle. Be brave. Be of ONE Spirit and yet of two, so separate and unique from one another. Strive to work together in harmony.

Saint Germain is asking us now to step back to a platform. He is touching our foreheads.

  Continue this transforming work of the inner knowledge, for the Brotherhood is most pleased with your work. And go with our blessing of light and the white dove. Amen.

He's placed on our foreheads his Violet Cross.

37

*Crystals help us to grow spiritually and
understand the God Source.*

Crystalline Structure
Saint Germain

It is Saturday morning and we are in Boise, Idaho. Tonight we have a presentation
for about twelve people at a metaphysical center. This trance session was originally
planned to receive specific information for this meeting, but for some reason
the Spiritual Teachers wanted to give in-depth instruction regarding crystals,
their classifications, and how they work with specific chakras. This is fascinating
information and apparently crystals can uniquely assist our ability to consciously
connect to the Elemental Kingdom.

*I told Saint Germain that I was tired this morning and he asked me to not be tired, that
there were many here ready to do work. He has in front of us a crystal.*

It's time to talk about the crystals themselves, what they mean and some of the
mysteries of unlocking them.

Now he's writing the word Velum.

This word is associated with the Veil you put on. The crystal structure has the
resonance to go beyond the Veil before your own radiance does. Within the
crystalline structure are layer upon layer of little points, points which focus energy.
Within even one given crystal, there could be up to ten thousand points and the
points have been programmed, each with a single thought, very much the way
you have etched onto discs, diskettes, for your computers for information that you
access. This is the exact same process that has happened to crystals, except the crystal
itself must be willing to accept the information. The Elemental Life Form must be
receptive. There are even some crystals which are not programmable. But the white
quartz, the clear, is the more receptive.

There are crystals which are specifically record keepers, record holders, and there are others that simply are of the Deva nature, Elemental nature. It's where the Elemental or Deva has voluntarily allowed the points to be programmed. We're speaking about the point itself as an eight-sided octagon, points leading out to both sides of the octagon. Inside the octagon itself, this pointed area, is a swirling activity on both sides which is sort of a flat plane to the center. This is the area of programming. It is a force. The thought is impressed or programmed through one end and the other end is the way in which the information is released.

Accessing a crystal is done through psychometry, allowing your energy to enter into the field of it to receive an impression. This can be done through many ways and the most simple form now being done is through the sense of touch. Yet in the future, it will be done through thought projection. As your consciousness expands, you will be able to access this information just through your finer body. Presently, this sensation of touch allows enough contact with this accessing spiral.

You see, Dear ones, it is the electromagnetic current which you set up which allows the finer energy to pass through the electrical field. The combination of using the Violet Ray and the Green Ray sets up this magnetism, an electromagnetic band. This is information which primarily goes through the Third Eye Chakra and accesses the higher mind, bringing it to the conscious recognition and into conscious activity.

Now, people feel that they are able to access much more readily, different ways of handling and different ways of touching. What they are doing is merely adjusting the piece to fit their field. Everyone's field is a little bit different. However, the highest way to read through the sensation of touch is through the point itself, for the point is generally the access key. The highest condensation of the spiraling energy is through that. In the case of the double terminated, you would want to put a finger on each one of the points. Now do you have questions?

Question: "Yes, in setting up this energy field to access a crystal, would we visualize the Blue and the Green Rays?"

Yes and also visualize them coming in through the Third Eye Chakra. This has been most beneficial to most students presently. Mankind's Third Eye has yet to be developed and opened to its fullest potential. The Violet and Green Ray appear to enhance and assist this opening.

Understand, this is a molecular structure within. The size is not the determination of a crystal's storability but only a determination of the power that it can generate. The larger the crystal is, and not by the number of points it contains, will create a more powerful force field in terms of power generation. Very small crystals can contain just as much information. In fact, you will find that some of the smaller crystals contain some of the highest truths, some of the more valuable information. But the larger ones are more simplistic in nature and are therefore some of the first to be programmed. The larger ones are also more simplistic in terms of duality, which at this point is an easier process for you to understand. We'll talk about this concept of duality.

There is the physical manifestation of a mineral from the Mineral Kingdom, the mineral freewill involved in passing and getting information and the actual crystalline structure which exists and allows this to happen. However, the dualistic nature we would like to explain here is that of polarity, of the magnetism itself. We have a negative and a positive. Some crystals are lying east/west and some are lying north/south and through the Deva or Elemental which they are associated with, those that lie north to south are more easily programmed for power sources, whereas, those that lie east to west are more easily programmed for informational purposes, for telecommunication. Do you understand this?

Question: "Crystals that are in columns within the ground, like in Orofino, Steptoe Butte, and above Boise, are these on end?"

Yes, many of them are. It would be good to check the direction of them. Many of these large crystal storehouses are some of the first crystals which were programmed by mankind in the early ages.

Question: "Were they placed there or were they there and then programmed?"

Some were placed, once man perfected this knowledge. Some are in a natural habitat. Later, as man progressed through the ages, he learned the actual structure, so now you have the synthetic creation of crystals. The natural ones contain the Deva energy working with them. The synthetic do not necessarily contain this Elemental energy; however, they do contain the points within which are still accessible and in some ways purer in form. However, those with the Deva element contained in them are more caring and more easily accessible. You may find that those which are synthetic in nature are more abrasive to your energy at this moment. It is the same as all things, that which is given by Nature and that which is a replica, made by mankind. In your society, you would have a fabric called silk and many women made silk stockings from this. Then you have the synthetic nylon. While nylon is a stronger fabric, it does not have the refinement of silk.

Question: "Is this a similar principle with crystal balls, the coarser crystals at this time are easier to read than the high quality crystal balls?"

They are more accessible in terms of the Deva elements, more accessible for mankind at his given radiation and vibration. There are those who are accessing the finer crystals. While I say finer, I can also say coarser in nature, yet finer in terms of their information and details to be released. Eventually, you will not need to access these at all, for they only contain information from other civilizations, some from Atlantis, some from Lemuria, some from civilizations which existed far before Lemuria. Others contain records from other planets. Yet, the Universal Source is all that is truly needed. It just appears that this is a way to assist mankind at the given moment.

Mankind has experienced life only through his sensational feeling of touch, seeing, and hearing and whether he knows it at this time, he is also hearing a vibration from these crystals. There will be a time when he will give this up, for it is not that necessary to have this in order to focus into this information. If he learns to become the clear open channel which he truly already is, these will not be needed. For some however, it is still of great assistance and benefit. There is much information to be unlocked and this is another key to what appears to be many mysteries, which are in truth, not mysteries at all.

Question: "What about the crystal I have been using?"

That particular crystal is synthetic in nature. It is a more difficult crystal to read. It is a much more powerful crystal than some of the more natural ones. There is not a particular Deva working with that crystal. Because it is a synthetic one, it has manifested itself, therefore it will take a particular amount of energy to unlock the Third Eye for that information to become totally accessible.

Response: "I had assumed that it was necessary on some level for my growth."

It is not that it is necessary, as much as you are drawn to it, the compatibility of vibration. It is much the same way you are drawn to people, from the way that they speak or look or talk. It is the vibration of where you are that gives you a feeling of compatibility. So it is with a gem.

Question: "Was it just the vibration of that crystal or was it my compatibility with the information I recognized at some level?"

It is the information you are accessing. Understand, there are the Beloved gems, those which beyond synthetic creation, come through precipitated creation, that which is the true soul nature of God. Those from the synthetic nature were manufactured and then programmed. Those from the precipitated nature are those which have come forth through Elemental command. This entailed the complete cooperation and constructive thinking between Elemental Life Form, the Mineral Kingdom and the Directive Force of the God Source brought through the command of man.

Response: "Lori and I have had visions of laboratories that we assume people were creating and programming crystals."

This is precisely what I am speaking to you about, these factories, as you would say. This was a period of time toward the end of Atlantis, when this power was greatly misused, specifically in synthetic manufacturing. You had the misuse of the precipitated crystalline structure, which had been brought forth to heal mankind. This was then used as a power source against mankind, a true adulteration of the law.

In the beginning, you had those of the Elemental nature, which brought forth the information and worked in a cooperative manner with mankind to bring this knowledge of the programmable points. Later on, there was total cooperation of the Devas in the synthetic construction and nature of these crystalline shapes. As man became aware of the great God Source within himself, he produced the crystalline shapes of the precipitated nature, those of the highest energies. Yet through his directed force, he then misused all of the energy within. This is much of the reason why mankind is being drawn to the crystalline shape at this time. In his most unconscious and subconscious activity, he is calling forth the purification of this Elemental Life Force. This Elemental Life Force will be released as man learns to let go of the need to manipulate a physical shape in order to understand the God Source energy.

Question: "The product you showed us that helps the crystals to get back to their basic programming or original intent, is that something that could help with the purification in general?"

This complete use of Violet Ray and Green Ray light projected together in the spiraling shape is very similar to the Tesla Coil. Edison was very aware of some of these principles. However, at the time, this was not allowed to be released into the conscious activity. Westinghouse has also been aware of this. While it was brought to the subconscious levels with both of these entities, it was blocked and stopped. There were other areas of growth that needed to expand within the actual Heart Chakra of mankind at the time, for the directive will of man is still scattered. They do not understand yet, the total concept of turning over of the will. El Morya has given you much instruction along this line and this is indeed a part of the instruction which is still very important.

Beloved Paul the Venetian has much work to do upon the Pink Ray for you and for the cleansing of the Heart Chakra and the emotional body, as you would know it. Archangel Michael has much work to do with you for the total purifying of the will and total purification of the vessel to remain clean, clear, and pure. This will put the directive force of God into right action and right use. I realize this is much for you to absorb at this moment and so I am leaving you now. I would like you to study the Vortex shape, the nature of dualistic polarity and understand the wavelengths of the colors I have given to you. Understand the crystalline shape. It is an important shape for understanding a programmable point.

Remember, we give you much to do. We keep you busy and we keep you active only in the constructive way. This will give you much to do, yes, in your spare time and keep you into the most constructive efforts of the highest nature. Remember, I AM yours for the transformation of this planet and I come to you with much joy, peace, and love.

38

Shower, cleanse, adjust, grow, and glow in the light!

Chamber of the Heart
Master Rada
Saint Germain

It is Monday and we have just left Boise. But before we leave and check out of our hotel, a new Spiritual Teacher appears—Master Rada. This is his instruction that is specifically focused upon the heart chakra and how we can quickly rejuvenate our emotional body while traveling and presenting this information. It is good to know that there are specific spiritual techniques that we can apply to re-adjust and balance our depleted energies. Afterwards, Saint Germain shares alchemic knowledge of the ONE. He assures us that even though the work ahead may be "trying," our spiritual thirst will be satisfied by our assimilation and trust of the experience.

There's another entity here today who is coming through and wants to speak.

Welcome chelas to the inner Chamber of the Heart, that of understanding the Initiation of the Heart Chakra, the Pink Ray of Divine Service to mankind.

He's wearing a kind of a pink and gold robe and he looks very Tibetan. Master Rada is his name. He is a messenger of the Pink Ray.

I've come to give you instructions on this work of the Heart Chakra, that which needs to be cleansed and brought into alignment for the acceleration of the times before you. Also, that of the emotional body, which needs to be brought into proper alignment and balance. For it is not proper that we align just the physical without also aligning the work of the subtle energies. I bring you this day the knowledge of this work, for as you travel about, you must understand that your emotional body is affected. As you weary and seek the need to go deep within yourself, we will instruct you in ways to make this adjustment finer. This will become less time consuming and have a greater ease of frequency.

First is the visualization technique. Stand with hands outstretched. From the left-hand side, see the light source flowing through the arm, circulating around the Heart Chakra, and out the right. Repeat this four times. Then through the Third Eye Chakra, visualize renewed light flowing through it and going directly to the Heart Chakra. As you visualize this light, see it flowing through the chakra from both sides, enveloping the center of the heart and cradling it in light. This is an uplifting visualization, uplifting to the emotional state. And now through the Crown Chakra, visualize sparks of violet light coming through like stars, surrounding and enveloping the body in a complete dazzling show of stars. As these stars enter into your cosmic field, they are showering and cleansing your system.

There are also some dietary needs which have to do with emotion: celery root, sassafras tea, orange peel, and ascorbic acid. These taken in supplemental quantities help to resist the fatigue of this chakra center, which is so easily drained in the service you do. Try this meditation and visualization I have given to you.

He's leaving now. He's leaving through something which looks like a pink rose. It's just sort of closing up. Saint Germain has returned and is holding up three fingers and asking us to visualize the Violet Flame around both of us at this moment and taking us to a table to sit for instructions. He has a box with him with a handle on the top. He's opening up the collapsible box. On the blackboard he is writing ENERGY DISBURSEMENT and underneath that word, REFRACTIONISM.

This is the fracture of the Elemental Molecular Source to create the needed effect for the equal distribution of energy. We need to discuss this principle. In front of you, I would like for you to take the simplest of forms, the triangle and the circle. You can fit a circle inside the geometric shape of the triangle with ease and flow, without distracting the shape of the triangle. And yet, this is impossible to do within the circle, of placing the triangular shape within the circle. You have a distracted flow, an abrasion, an inefficient use of plane energy. So how is this dispensed to flow fluidly? We must bond the geometric shapes to one another. So we enter into the Theory of Harmonic Balance. Do we change the shape of one to adjust to the other? No. Remember the spiritual principle: As above, so below. So what do we do? We find a way to bond them to each other. And so we develop the Theory of Dimension and allow the two shapes to parallel one another.

So visualize, if you will, the triangular shape and the circular shape overlapping each other, dimensionally parallel. And then visualize the rotation of the shapes. At first, you may have a rotational pull, one going one way, one going the other. Or, they may both be rotating in the same direction. The rotational axis is in the center and is the point of the fusion or bonding of two parallel rotating shapes. So, soon we do not have the disharmony and have the bonding of energies regardless of the way they flow. If one is running counter clockwise, the other clockwise, the intersection of the axis rotation at .287 revolutions per millisecond is the pattern to form a bonding. Where is the bond? The center. As these two shapes twist and turn, a point of contact occurs and the inner action of the shapes becomes one shape. This is the point of implant or impact.

With molecular implantation, we have one of the highest principles of geometric function. Shape is not limited, for shape is that which is ready for change. And the recognition of linear shape is truly the recognition of linear change. As these two shapes merge to become one, we have a molecular explosion at the point of contact. From the two, the third is derived and spun off again from the point of the axis. Do you have any questions?

Question: "Is this also a visualization for blending our chakras into ONE?"

Yes, this principle is intact in all life forms and yet, I am explaining this so that you will understand the principles of energy refraction. If you take two shapes, moving in simultaneous harmony, in the same force of direction, what do you get? The two become one. Now, you would wonder, what is best, merging as one or merging for creative activity? It will depend largely upon the desired result, for if you need to create a substance such as water or heat, as we have talked about with this device, there are times when you will need to dissipate such energy, to bring it back to recycle for reuse.

Now, as you begin to understand simple structures, such as the triangle and the circle and how to meld their shapes for the desired result, we will begin work again upon this project. I wish for you to understand this principle in its clearest form, for as we come to more complicated shapes, you will need to understand directional gravitational pulls along this axis. Yes, there are many ways that this can be used for healing but our focus is primary upon structure and shape at this given moment.

Question: "So, is this a parallel concept to breaking down white light into the various colored bands and back again and also breaking water down into the hydrogen/oxygen and back again?"

Yes, we are talking about the interaction of two to become one or two to equal desired effect. And yet, we are talking about one principle. Remember, Beloved chelas, this may seem like a trying work ahead of you and yet if you will continue to drink from the cup, the lessons which we gently guide you through, you will no longer thirst. You will see with brilliance what the human eye cannot. You will experience light through a sensation you have never experienced previously. The riches of this Kingdom are at your disposal. So do not fear, do not give up. But trust. This goes beyond trying. This enters into the trusting relationship we have as you sit at this desk, as you do the things in the simple manner in which we present. Master Rada has come to give you what you have needed and our work will continue and grow and glow in this light. Give praise and thanks to your Beloved Mighty I AM Presence, through whose patience and love this work continues.

[Editor's Note: Master Rada is currently incarnate in Third Dimension in the lower mountains of Tibet. He is most expert in the techniques he described. *The Life and Teachings of the Masters of the Far East* by T. Baird Spalding describes this.]

39

*Develop harmony and faith—it just may help you
to avoid the common cold!*

A Body of Light
Saint Germain

Before we continue on our trip, we return home for a few days. With the stress of organizing our schedule, two quick trips to both ends of Idaho State, and planning everything before we leave, Dan catches a nasty cold. In this session, Saint Germain bathes Dan's energy field with healing light and gives suggestions to hasten the healing process. The diagnosis is interesting: apparently too much fixation on the rational mind is akin to "lowering the vibration to second-dimension." The cure: spiritually work to attain balance and harmony within through developing faith. And remember, "I AM with you and will guide you and assist you."

Saint Germain is here and I've asked him if we could practice his healing technique with you.

Before we start, focus on the healing light, the healing Green Ray. Run this light first from the bottom of the feet up through to the top of the head. And run it at least twelve times, each time visualizing it charging all of your systems and sustaining you in perfect health and wellness. As you recognize the energy running, feel the pulsation. It pulses through your system much as the circulatory system pulsates. This is a similarity in healing, that you must visualize the substance going through your system much as the blood runs through the veins. You currently have a viral infection. You must first see the structure of that which has inhabited your system.

He's showing that to me now. It looks a little like a pyramid on two sides, joined together with an odd circle toward the center and an offshoot on the end.

As you see what has invaded your system, you must ask for its removal to the highest cause, your I AM Presence.

143

AM HEALTHY AT ALL TIMES.
ONE WITH MYSELF AT ALL TIMES.
I AM AT PEACE.
HE PUREST LIGHT TO RUN THROUGHOUT MY
SYSTEM.
I ASK AT ALL TIMES
FOR THE REMOVAL OF ANYTHING WHICH CAUSES DISHARMONY
OR DISCORD IN THE FUNCTIONING OF MY SYSTEM.
MY BODY IS TRULY THE HIGHEST EXPRESSION OF LIGHT
AND I WILL CONTINUE EXPRESSING MY BODY AS A BODY OF LIGHT.

If you will continue to do this periodically throughout the day, recognizing that your body is truly a body of healing light, there will be no need for this encounter with this vibratory level. For you see, what has truly happened is that you have made contact with the Second Dimension. Disease actually comes from contact with Second Dimension, a vibratory level you are not accustomed to. You have taken on something common at that state of consciousness. Therefore, you have entities in physical embodiment who vibrate at that consciousness, the cellular animals you call a virus. Their conscious level vibrates at a certain frequency and when combined with human emotion and the human will, the cellular animals are directed in the path of the human energy they encounter.

If mankind could only know, it is through no mistake that disease comes into his physical body. It happens through contact on the conscious level. Much as we contact you in the physical by lowering our vibrations, in this case of disease, you have lowered your vibration and contacted that of a lower form of physical expression. However, in this case of this organism, it has caused disharmony with your system.

That of the emotional body is also involved, for you see, the emotional body also has its layers of consciousness. Much as the conscious mind itself has its layers of consciousness, so does the emotional body. And what you experience are slips, brief slips into these periods. It is through this work that we work to raise you out of this and keep you in constant balance and harmony. For those experiencing the physical, it is indeed the task to keep the level of faith. The reason there is always a lull before the storm is so that those who say the wind blows this way can have the opportunity to blow the cloud away. Remember I AM with you and will guide you and assist you.

Saint Germain is coming closer now. Did you feel that? My hands are just electric.

40

*All journeys are inevitably about the
inner journey—the spiritual experience.*

Journal of Light
Master of Oneness
Saint Germain
El Morya

It is Sunday morning, and today we leave on our trip. So the first entry is our final instruction. I am filled with excitement, but Dan has some fears, and rightly so. When we return he will still face financial pressures that will not disappear overnight. In juxtaposition with this worry is the light and encouragement from the Spiritual Teachers and their remembrance of our divinity, courage, and the promise of opportunity.

This lesson contains five entries from different sessions with the Spiritual Teachers as we traveled through Washington, Oregon, and northern California. Entry Two was received in Klamath Falls, Oregon, where we presented the I AM America Map to a large group at the Unity Church. Entry Three, received in Carmel, California, is an insightful lesson on the relationship of human consciousness to the probability of Earth Changes. Entry Four continues along this same vein of thought and presents how our individual perceptions along with our mental state contribute to the mass consciousness of Earth. This lesson was received on a beautiful morning in Ojai, California. Entry Five is continued guidance for Dan's health, which was still not 100 percent.

As we traveled through the western states, we stopped in numerous bookstores throughout Oregon and California. The Map was well received, and many commented about its beautiful design and radiant energy. Here are the transcripts from our travels and the resplendent inner journey, with the masterful tour guides: Saint Germain, Master of Oneness, and El Morya.

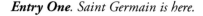

Entry One. *Saint Germain is here.*

Welcome chelas of the Grand Order, for you come for instruction again. And I give this to you. It is the celebration of life that you rejoice in the power of the I AM Activity. It is the ONE true way, the ONE true source of All That Is. By this power, you shall know the ONE true being. By this power, you shall know all that there is to know. For you wonder about the mysteries of life and the mysteries on this planet and there are no mysteries, for all that ever will be is contained within the words I AM. Remember this throughout your travels. As you leave today on this trip, remember that the I AM is the largest and biggest gift of all which can be given to you. Keep this focus at all times and remember I AM with you and now walk with me.

We're walking down this path. He's just picked a peach from a tree.

Remember when I brought you here before and we picked this fruit and cut it open and inside, I showed you the pit and within the pit, the kernel. And now, I want you to focus upon the tree from which this fruit comes. For the true fruit of labor comes from the tree with its roots planted firmly. And its roots are planted firmly within the soil of truth. And the truth is the I AM. This can bring you the manifestation of all that you need. You do worry much about your money situation and truly, is this not only the exchange of energy? So as you travel, see this as only the exchange of your energy. Use the I AM to produce the finest results for bringing into manifestation all that you need.

Each day that you arise, bless this Presence and say:

I AM HEALTHY, I AM OPULENT, I AM A WELL BEING,
I AM READY TO RECEIVE THAT WHICH GOD HAS INTENDED
FOR ME TO HAVE THIS DAY,
I AM A DIVINE BEING, ONE CENTERED WITHIN THIS UNIVERSE,
I AM A SERVANT, I AM A TRUE MESSENGER OF TRUTH.

And remember this at all times, that you truly are a child of this universe and your parent will provide for you at all times. Should you feel short of money at any time say:

I AM COMMANDING THE UNIVERSE
TO PROVIDE FOR ME THIS INSTANT
AND TO SHOW ME THE CLEAREST PATH.

And doors will unfold for you. Remember this, for this is one of the hardest burdens to overcome and yet the I AM Activity and the use of this will give to you the gold from the Kingdom.

You have my blessings children, for recall when I was your parent and you set out on similar journeys before within the desert. You traveled with this message of light to share. And again I bless you. Continue to do the work, for it is of the highest order and trust that I AM with you, for I will present those within your path which you should encounter. There is a lady presently in Mount Shasta whom you shall meet and she will further your instruction in this activity. I'm opening up the floor now for you to ask questions. I AM here for your service and direction.

Response: "I feel good about the trip. I guess where my fears are coming in are when we return and I have money pressures."

The door will open from which this will be taken care of. It may take a period of six months to a year to clear from your books, but a door will open and you will clearly see the right path for you to take. Do not worry about this, as you will take care of this and you must have trust in yourself! Continue in your work and activity of the Brotherhood. Search and seek our activity, for there is much work for us all to do in this great cleansing and upliftment of the planet.

The belts around Earth are still muddied and yet there is the light which is starting to flicker and glow closest to the surface. One of the brightest spots where it is starting to manifest is close within your region. Take this light and spread it and share it with others. Bring to them this knowledge, that you can do all that you need to do and want to do working from universal substance, precipitating the spiritual into the physical. Master of Oneness is here and would like permission to speak.

Response: "Yes."

Beloved hearts of the Inner Fire, I come to bring you news of the Initiation of Earth. For yes, this spark of Divinity has begun to flow and it pulsates from the inner core. A great work this has been, for it has not been the work of just one but many who have sent their love to this planet. And from this great spark, you too may draw upon this energy source, for as you have given to Terra, you too can receive from the Mother.

I have given you the lion, the staff of the lion, whose symbol means strength and courage. Draw upon this for your Initiation. From your Navel Chakra and also from the Throat Chakra, visualize the Divine white cord running to the spark of energy, the belt of energy around Earth at this present moment. You will grow and learn, develop and obtain much strength from this universal substance. You must learn to speak this truth and do it with courage and with the strength of all that you are. For have you not sprung from the loins of a force greater than yourself? You are indeed the Divine Inheritors of this Kingdom. You are the Prodigal Son and you have a right to partake of this universe.

On your trip Dear ones, remember that at all times, that you are indeed Sons of God, that you are indeed the Divine Inheritors and let no one tell you that you are not. For you truly are and my blessings and protection go with you. I give you this symbol, the lion. It's in a diamond-type shape. Wear it close to your heart and remember the courage and strength which you can draw from it. I will continue my work with you and verse you in meditation, universal law, and Initiation. Be willing to share the information, for this work cannot be complete if it is hoarded only by the few. This work is only complete when it is dispensed to all and brought to the light. For is this not Oneness that we understand, pure universal Oneness? And pave the pathway for the Great Age upon us. Blessings to you, Keepers of the Heart Flame. Love and opportunity await you, Beloved children.

This is Saint Germain. Bless you and wear the cloak of your Divinity at all times. Keep your focus strong, anchored not only within your heart but in that which is above you and surrounds you. See in others what you see in yourself. Truly look for that which is the Christ in all. Look not with judgment upon them and rejoice in all the work that you do. As you spread this message, we will continue our work.

Entry Two. *I just opened up the channel to Saint Germain. He is very close to us and has been traveling with us on this trip.*

My consciousness will be very close to you all throughout the trip, for the completion of this project is essential. Beyond being essential, it is an important work that you have not learned to value yet. This will be realized as you progress. You see Dear ones, this is a project which goes beyond the reasoning of human economics and cannot be valued by money. Live in love and balance during this trip.

And when you feel fatigued, remember I AM there. And you may reach your hand out to me and I will extend mine in loving response.

Question: "What do you need to share with us today and what directions do you have?"

There are three important stops today for you and I will assist you in finding them. One in particular will prove to be a very important connection for you in this work. For you know, this area is like a war zone. And throughout this day, keep your protection around you, for there are many thoughts and many entities which travel in this area. Beloved Archangel Michael will be here and you may call upon him for protection and call upon the Beloved Archangel Gabriel to give you guidance. And I will stay with you

I would like to verse you too on your diet. Take in only that which is pure and clean, for the stress of the many vibrations are hard upon the physical vehicle. At the end of your day, spend time in solitude and meditation to cleanse your system from this. Put only the freshest and most valuable foods to your system. Before you eat, charge them with a directed activity of the I AM, for are you not taking in that which is of the ONE Source? Recognize this in all that you do. And are you not taking in of the ONE Source as you travel and people are placed in your path? See that, as they give to you, you also give to them.

Question: "How can I be of service to you?"

Wear my cross throughout this day. Meditate on the points of the Maltese Cross. Draw your resonance into the center of its being, for this is the meditation of transformation. Remembering, there is a directed force which pulls you to the center.

Question: "Is my back problem just my kidneys acting up?"

I'm glad you have directed your question toward health, for your stirring hostilities are seeking emergence to the surface and you must ask daily for the Violet Flame for their removal. Each day, ask for the assistance of the members of the Ancient of Days and say this:

I INVOKE THE ASSISTANCE OF THE VIOLET FLAME.
I AM A BEING OF THE VIOLET FLAME,
CLEANSED IN THE HARMONY OF ALL THAT .

Each day, remember where you came from and remember this is your journey Home. And as you call to this Violet Flame, it is the source for you to remember, for you are both on this leg of your journey. And it will not be long Dear ones. I send my love and warmest wishes and regards.

Entry Three. Saint Germain starts this lesson with an explanation of consciousness and its movement out of fear and into spiritual enlightenment.

I will give you the following scale: at one end, one out of every five people are awakened. At the other end, one out of every two are awakened. Now, which seems the most weighted? Actually the five over one. What seems the safest? Naturally two over one and yet the two over one is the most extreme, for this creates polarization. Do you have any questions?

Question: "Is this shift happening sooner because of the rise in the consciousness of mankind?"

Yes, there is a possibility this may occur sooner. That is why you were given this period of time to complete this project, for it was a possibility we were concerned with. We are looking at a portion of mass consciousness to mass. We are talking about overall consciousness, the pulsating beat of thoughts, of those in harmony and those discordant. A rise in consciousness is not necessarily a rise in good thinking. It is a rise in balanced thinking. For you see, many perceive a shift in the poles as imbalance; whereas, in a more correct nature, we should say it is an act of balancing, of fine-tuning, of bringing Earth in harmony with the thoughts of harmony and balance.

And yes, as you suspect, there is that fine line at the last moment. There are those who are terrified and those who accept. Let us look at it this way, there is your fable of the slow turtle and that of the rabbit, the hare. And who gets there? The one who stays in balance, the one who is not harried, the one who does not run but seeks to understand the journey, the race as you might call it. But it is truly not a race, for a race would indicate competition and that is not the nature of this work. It is a path. And yes, you do have the rabbit and the turtle both completing the race but it is the nature of their being that you should observe as they cross the line. Do we run with a frantic push or do we endure? For we know we are guided and directed. Do we run as if to hide or do we push onward on the path? For we know it is the path. Do we hop over that which we cannot accept or do we accept the obstacle in the path and patiently wait for the removal? For we understand that it is still the path. Remember, Dear ones, harmony and balance. Be patient.

He's taking my hand and we're walking through a portal. Give me your hand … do you feel the energy?

Beloved one, do not fear…

Entry Four. *Both Saint Germain and El Morya are present and quite strongly. To the back of them is yet another Master Teacher. They would like to give us instructions on the use of the mental Vortex. They're showing a swirling activity and as you look down into it, you can see the great vacuum it creates. They are holding their hands toward it, sending two energies up into it. This teaching has something to do with tornados.*

Again, Dear ones, this is a cleansing activity of the Elementals, brought to cleanse the mental bodies of mankind. While you perceive much suffering and much death, what is truly happening is the cleansing, not only of Earth but of the mental and emotional bodies of man. We are talking about the mass consciousness, the mass mental abilities of all mankind.

Perception is the key. You must learn to perceive each moment as the gift that it truly is. You must learn to perceive each moment to be filled with life and love for one another. If you would like to perceive destruction, then that is truly what you then can have. But through the gift of the mind, you can switch this. You can make the choice. Much as you would turn a light on and off, you can decide how you will perceive each moment. Will you perceive it in the light, a natural progression of things that truly are, or will you perceive with agitation, perceive with destructive thoughts, perceive with discordant energy?

As your perceptions come to you, remember this is your chance to practice the highest spiritual principles. As your perceptions come to you, this is the way you interact in the physical. Your physical perceptions are what you perceive while in the physical embodiment. Your spiritual perceptions are what you perceive while in the spiritual. So let's examine both of these. You have your spiritual perceptions, that which comes to you through visions, intuition, and at night when you sleep. And then you have your physical perceptions, the conversations with people, the visual, speech, hearing, and all the senses which allow you to perceive through your physical vehicle. But now, we must look at the Third Eye Perception, that of the true inner sight and the inner hearing and inner sound. As you perceive an event which has come to you in the physical, you must first perceive it in this higher way, this higher dimension. Beloved El Morya is here to instruct you on the use of right perception, the use of mind and the right use of will.

Greetings, chelas. I come to you with information on the use of the mind and the will. We are talking about this information from a Third Dimensional perspective, of that which you cannot see and yet sense and process. We are talking specifically on the order of events and beyond the order of the outcome, for you must be able to stand back as the third person in any event which is happening, of which you are participating. This is truly the Third Dimension, detaching away from the conversation, detaching away from all that you sense in the physical and seeing it truly through the Third Eye. We can clearly define some perceptions as logical perceptions and some perceptions as intuitive perception. But now, let's talk about the right use of the mind, for its true home is that which comes from the force of merging intuitive logic, intuitive wisdom, and intuitive perception with love. These are bonded together through this synthesis called love. I would like to explain this further.

He's drawing a triangle.

We have at one pillar, Intuition; we have at the other, Perception. And the point at the top is the third, the Third Eye of which we speak. It is bringing these to the clear focus, to the center, the balance which is the truth, the true use of the right mind for right perception. You deal with those who have a denser, heavier emotional body and who have a denser, heavier ego body. For while we have emotional bodies, we also have the ego body, which comprises a denser, thicker substance from the wrong use of the mind activity. Through the use of the Third Eye perception, we come to understand how we can shed the ego body and bring into balance the emotional body, keeping an alignment through right use and right perception. I AM El Morya, who works upon this Wisdom Ray.

Today throughout your travels, as you are introduced to higher truths, remember to stand back as the third person. Remember to stand back and detach and perceive clearly through your Third Eye. Look at this with the right perception for you. Remember the energy vortices at the beginning of this discourse? This is the way to keep yourself clean, to keep your aural substance from adhering to that which is unneeded or unwanted. Stand back without judgment but know within yourself. Perceive this not through ego; perceive this not through emotion. Stand back.

I hand to you this day, a gold key, truly the key to all the Wisdom of the Ages. It's never that which is locked, for true wisdom was never lost. True wisdom is that which needs not to be found but it is that which is discovered and always in existence. You Dear chelas must be prepared to stand back as the third person, utilizing Divine Wisdom, Divine Perception through right use of the mind and the will. Call to me and I will answer you. Call to me and this key is here at all times.

Saint Germain says thank you as El Morya stands aside.

Initiates, continue to use your meditations of Violet Fire and continue to ask for the protection of Archangel Michael. I AM with you always.

Entry Five. *Saint Germain is here.*

We would like to discuss dietary needs with you and that of your respiratory illness. You need a higher elevation of sunlight and meditation in the sun. For this truly will bring you back to your level of harmony. And of course, what you should know is that your dosage of Vitamin D comes naturally through the layers in sunlight. And you are lacking in the mineral called chromium. Did you want to ask any questions?

Question: "How do I obtain this mineral?"

This is a trace mineral found alongside what you would call Vitamin A. However, it is much more specific. It is found in certain beans on your planet, in brown rice and any kind of vegetable that is a deep leafy green. Spinach, chard, or anything that has a deep green to it, almost more of a purplish green but not cabbage. You also need a trace of magnesium in your system. Cut back on your dosages of Vitamin C and get in the sunlight to adjust your level of consciousness. Also, do the meditations when you are in the sun; this will be the most uplifting thing for you to do, aside from your diet. I will come through to assist in the healing. On the deepest level, you have lost some faith. While I cannot restore it to you, I can work to bring you back to balance, if this is what you wish.

Response: "Yes."

Remember I AM with you and will guide you and assist you!

41

Transformation and the New Times

Six Pivot Points

Saint Germain
El Morya
Sananda

We arrived in Phoenix several days before Thanksgiving after spending a week in Los Angeles. During that time, we stayed with Dan's sister and we had an amazing visit to the Whole Life Expo where we networked the Map and received many new contacts. I had a reading with a well-known psychic reader and she told me that I was involved in work similar to hers—I guess she meant "psychic work." She said my career had just begun and would be inordinately long—that is, I would be involved for many years with helping people to understand the unseen worlds. She said that I would return to Los Angeles many, many times! [Fast forward to the future: this is accurate.]

One night I went to bed early so Dan could visit with his sister. The next day he seemed remote and wanted to leave. I was a bit frustrated by his sullen behavior—we were invited to stay for Thanksgiving. Maybe the schedule and his nagging cold were getting to him.

We traveled to Phoenix in a day and by dusk had checked into a motel on the western edge of the Valley. I awoke early in the morning and the air was invitingly warm, so I dove into the pool for a morning swim. Coming up for air, I immediately noticed a cloud formation in the perfect appearance of a Phoenix. I took this to be a good sign, as I knew we were located on the outer perimeters of the Golden City of Gobean. Later that morning I received this lesson about the Phoenix and Mesa areas along with prophecies about their unique purpose in the New Times.

〰

We are in Phoenix, and Saint Germain and El Morya are present. El Morya is very tall, about seven feet tall and wearing a white turban. Since this is the area where he will be focusing his work, he would like to speak.

My work is that of the transformation of the soul. The true transformation of the soul is integration. Inner harmonies work within the self and beyond the self to become the total integration with that of the Source. I would like to explain this to you. There are six portions to the integrated self, each corresponding to six Chakra Centers. Each of these correspond with six layers of the human auric field and the same of Earth.

At times you may be experiencing more strongly the Initiation of the Fifth Path or the Fourth Path in a direct lesson, and then you are initiated into this specific path. Soon, these paths are interwoven. Lessons from the fourth go to lessons from the second or lessons from the third interweave with lessons from the fifth. Initiation is the pathway of discerning, fine-tuning each lesson to experience the universal principle. And at all times, understanding that you are just as you are. As it was said I AM THAT I AM. This is true Initiation.

So you have the six energy points lining up on the meridian. In this area, our focus is with the completing of these energies, bringing them into total balance and directed at the third and second chakras. We work to bring the body and the soul and surrounding energies to this path of transformation. Is it not through action that this occurs?

He is pointing to Balance, Love, Wisdom, and utilizing these energies as Action to bring forth Transformation.

This will be an area of dense population and people interacting in a most harmonious fashion, learning that the path is right action. Do you have questions?

Question: "Would you show me the points?"

In this area at the point of Mesa, a base command will be set up. Higher technologies will come into this area for the balancing of the mind. Much work will be done in this area for criminal justice. Much technology will be brought here for the balancing of those of the criminal mind, for it is only that their energies are out of alignment. We will set up six centers within this area for treatment of those termed criminally insane and bring them back to the highest form of God use and impeccable character. Many will see these as treatment centers but they are beyond that of a treatment. Divine Intervention will be allowed to occur and then they can make their choice of whether or not to remain in embodiment. They may remain only with the finer adjustments.

You must understand that we are truly concerned with the welfare of all involved. Those of the criminal mind who cannot make this finer adjustment into this New Age must be treated or removed. We assure you, we will work hard and long hours before any final decision is made for the removal of such a soul.

For a period of time, many will call this a valley of sorrow, a valley of much weeping. And yet, it will be raised to become that of the highest joy and transformation, for from here will spring the true enlightened race, that which will understand the mysteries of the interaction of energies. For in human relationships, we are dealing with the finer substance of the Human Aura and this knowledge will be brought into the application of the greatest light. Many of you adjust your energy frequencies through meditation, physical activity, and/or social interaction, which raise or lower your vibration. This energy is brought by the vibratory forces, the magnetic forces determining interaction. This will be an area where the laws of interaction will be examined thoroughly.

There is also specific work to do with children, particularly bringing this knowledge to be used in the beginning levels. For you see, if we recognize energetic movement from the start of embodiment, the soul moves with much ease and understands interaction with the higher levels of the directive forces.

Many will come here to transcend racial issues. I will work specifically on the directed Ray of Wisdom in this area, with the finer use of the will and highest spiritual truth remaining the focus and the use of right action through the finer use of the auric bodies. Do you have any questions?

Question: "Is there anything you want to share with our group tomorrow?"

I would like to share the information of the pivot points. There are six in this area. These six pivot points will be used to build the base. Much technology will be released in many forms, for it shall be through the right use of the mind, integrated with action, which will bring transformation and unity to the human soul. This is indeed a planet of peace.

Question: "Would you explain the six pivot points?"

There are the pivot points of the chakras but there are also pivot points which are actual geographic locations. The pivot points which are in use at this moment will become further activated to reinforce the network. These are energy points which have been anchored in the sixth field or body of the Earth Planet. You see, this activity has long been going on in this area. Many are aware of it and yet, only aware on such a subtle level. Intergalactic travel is something that you humans dream of and we know is thoroughly possible but this will not be allowed until you respect the use of the mind through right action. Take heart, there are those who will soon be ready to open to this vast technology which we hope to share with you. Dear ones, the strides are being made slowly but surely. But there are many among you who hold the work back. We will continue with our plans.

I am in a garden with Saint Germain and Sananda. Saint Germain is speaking.

Welcome to the garden. Together we take you here for rest and relaxation and give to you a discourse on inner harmony. What is inner harmony but meditation on the soul? And what is the soul but that which is the seed and the Source? And so, as you calm yourself and meditate upon that which is the true Source, do you not see that which is the seed of yourself, the soul? At times you feel disjointed, irregular, pieced and patched together and yet you must collectively draw your energies into this one Source. Feel it as it anchors within your heart. Then anchor your energies within, what you call, the pineal gland located in the center of the brain and then up through the top of the head. You must spend at least five minutes of your calculated time in reference to this state, for this state harmonizes the inner bodies, the finer bodies. Yes, you have among you the inner bodies which are the chakra points and the outer bodies which correspond to that of electromagnetic field.

As you understand the planet itself, you too shall understand the creation of your own bodies. Do you not have in the planet, the inner core and layers? Each are corresponding to substance and to the Elemental Life Force. And to the outside of Earth itself, do you not have atmospheric layers? Such is the composition too of your body. And then we contact the Source, that which is within the heart, the fiery seed of which all substance is composed. The fiery seed unites the spiritual and the physical. This is the same structure you find in all physical matter and the same vibratory force which you find in all spiritual matters.

This fiery seed is indeed the link between the spiritual and the physical, its composition resting on twelve sides (twelve points, thirteen facets) and yet octagon in shape. While we can structurally break this apart so you may understand this on a material basis, our highest endeavor is for you to understand this as a wave on the spiritual side. All energy is conducted upon this wave and all action is created upon this wave. It serves as the link for the actions of the God activities manifesting and then returning to the Source from whence it came. Now Sananda would like to speak.

This valley is indeed the area where we set the six pivot points, not only for the disbursement of energies from other galaxies but also for the planet. As you prepare for these Earth Changes, realize the transformation of your soul is of the utmost importance, for it is indeed the highest message. The essential ingredients given for the transformation of the soul are compassion, sharing, giving, and loving. All of these you are aware of but all of these you may forget when carrying the limited shell of the physical. Transform your being, for that truly cannot be destroyed. Lift yourself to me for my assistance.

Understand the vibratory action of compassion as a quality of the heart. Learn to give without receiving. This is indeed a lesson many experience and this path, while at times seems to be the hardest to climb, it is that which gives the most assured success. As the Golden Age is ushered in, you must prepare this path, for this is the path that we too have travelled upon. And it is with our hope that we will travel upon this path with you and in ministry to you. Open up this gateway, so that we can be of assistance to you and you to us, for as you speak of the work you do with us, it is the life that you lead which clearly shows to others the nature of your work. It is by your actions, which others look to you and approve or disapprove. It is through you that they feel the radiance of the Masters to come. Yes, there will be the thrill seekers, those who wish to see. And then there are truly those who tread the path through sincere effort.

Break bread with your Brothers. Commune with your Brothers. Remember, they too struggle on this path. Is this not compassion, seeing that which you have seen in yourself? Even if you may not be currently manifesting that particular experience, search within yourself. Remember, as you see this in others, how you too have felt and then brought your energies into balance and awareness.

He's holding his hand out.

Reach to me. Remember, I too was once where you are. As I hold my hands out to you, this is the bridge. Hold your hands to your Brothers, for you too are a bridge. And is not this transformation, true use of compassion? Contemplate on giving and sharing. Remember the true use of your energies.

42

Earth Change is also spiritual and dimensional change.

Center of Inner Sight

Saint Germain

Our presentation in Phoenix had one of the highest turn-outs, but the best was yet to come. Dan and I had heard about Sedona from friends but had never been there and its striking red rocks and vivid blue sky welcomed us. We knew no one; however, our hunch was that this was the place for us to give yet another presentation of the Map. Through talking to one bookstore clerk after another and through a series of "friend-of-a-friend" meetings, we met Andrew, aka "Miracle Worker."

In less than three hours he networked, made telephone calls, and efficiently arranged for a lecture of the I AM America Map in his home—and it was packed. There must have been over sixty people at the informal presentation and, to this day, Andrew remains one of my beloved friends.

We spent several days in Sedona, hiking and taking in the breathtaking landscape. One morning I awoke and knew it was time to receive a new lesson. Here is Saint Germain's insight on Sedona and its purpose throughout the changes and into the New Times.

He has the map out on the chalk board and is using a pointer.

I realize that you've had very many questions about this trip and I'm prepared to start answering some of the specific questions if you'd like to ask.

Question: "What is to become of Sedona? Will it be an island or is its purpose over?"

Most people would prefer to see their area stay and there will be more of an inlet formed in this area. And yes, there will be a lot of island activity, for the Vortex areas need to rest for awhile. Their purpose has been to serve as portals of exchange between the dimensions.

Question: "So some of the mountains will remain around here but will they be connected to the main coast?"

The inlet area is connected to the main body but there will be dozens of small islands protecting the small bay. The bay is in the shape of a horseshoe. Sedona is that of an island, surrounded by smaller islands. This will form pockets, allowing for isolated activities of the other dimensions. This isolation is intended for non-destructive purposes and for protection, for long the truths have come from this source and this has been a center of great truth for much of mankind.

It is the intent of the Brotherhood to protect that which has served well, for you see, Dear ones, as these changes occur, many people will flock to these centers. Since many people who are not yet initiated on the Wisdom Ray may adulterate the true teachings, there will be a geological barrier placed around this area. But beyond, there will be the centers that will serve on the coastline to the Sedona area, to service the many people who will wish to come to experience the portals. There will be some who will run here hoping to leave the area and yet will find a truer intention.

In this area, be prepared to see many centers of light opening on the mainland into this horseshoe pocket I have shown you. Many people will regard this area as a transportation center to the higher truths. Yet, if one is not aligned and prepared within his heart, it will not be acceptable for him to physically travel to this area. And so nature has cooperated with the command the Mother herself has requested, for this area is a great nerve center of the inner sight. This area has served as a great point, aligned with Third Eye Chakra activity for the Earth's Being. Do you have any questions?

Question: "Should we be open about this?"

For those who request the information, you may share. But you yourself must learn the technique of those who ask, for remember we do not infringe upon the free will and this is your example. If you are asked for information, you may freely give it, for it is released upon the Ray of Truth and Sincerity. But to give it out and cast it among the public is to open it up for discussion. That would, to some, impede upon the free will. Do you understand?

Question: "Yes. Can you explain further our interaction with the geographical areas we've traveled to?"

Dear heart, we are talking much of physiology and how physiology is interrelated with the Spirit Body, drawing to itself that which is itself. As you've traveled with each other and felt Earth's energies and drawn upon the waters of those areas, taken the mineral and Deva activity of each area, you find within yourself that which is harmonizing and that which is nonharmonizing. You find that which is needed within the system to create balance, for you too are aligning your energy force-field. Have you not felt this in areas you have traveled to, that which is harmonizing to yourself?

Response: "Yes."

As we explained the seventh layer of the outer body, known as the integrated layer, you are drawing from the six outer bodies to assist the outer seventh. And from the outer seventh body, the conical shape begins to form. This field draws the Higher Self closer to integration.

He has drawn this out and it looks like an inverted cone shape.

For you see, you have that of the Spirit Body and the responding physiology. You have the densification, which is the precipitated result of what has been taken in through the outer bodies. As you travel to areas and take in energy through all the bodies in a specific geological area, the energy of some other entities in embodiment and also not in embodiment are drawn to you and assist you in harmonizing energies, which are then drawn into the seventh body.

Again, we are speaking of the cellular structure of the twelve and eight, which interrelates the Third to the Fourth Dimension. In the simplest terms, as you travel geologically to an area, you are gathering up the energies within yourself from the inner core and harmonizing to the outer. This too is a cleansing process. I will assist you in the mathematics of this but spend your time, Dear one, in the contemplation of this theory. If you have further questions, I would be willing to assist you.

Question: "The one thing most people have a hard time understanding are the weather patterns, specifically, why the northwest will become hot and tropical?"

They must understand the Earth Changes which will occur throughout other areas of the world. There will be an overall warming tendency throughout the planet.

Question: "Do you have any suggestions for our presentation?"

We are pleased presently at the way this information is presented. You will continue to act as servants in dispensing this information. Remember, we will draw to you those who are meant to hear this information, for this has a domino effect. We will direct and draw those to the information and they will share the information with those that they are drawn and directed to. This is not an action of force. Remember, Dear one, this is an activity of love, not only for the planet but love of the self. This is the path to be taken in the New Age.

43

The I AM America Map won't be the only one!

The New Times
Saint Germain

This is another lesson that was received in Sedona; it addresses personal questions concerning government and food production during and after the Time of Change. This lesson also contains unique information regarding government study of Earth Change.

Saint Germain is in front of the map.

I see that you have come with questions.

Question: "Our friend R.D. wanted us to ask what his new direction will be?"

To help the unfoldment of the new civilization to come. His focus is as a political leader, studying and analyzing the structures through which human beings interact with one another in the least imposing way. There will be a police state and during that time, there will be the underground network which will keep the order among those who truly thirst for freedom.

Dear ones, do not hesitate with fear when you hear about police action, for what we are speaking of is police action taken in the hands of the people themselves. We see a period of time where there will be no one cohesive government and who should the burden of responsibility fall to? Upon the people. And there is a period of time where the consciousness will not yet be raised and thus you will get the interaction of the police state. It is therefore the responsibility of those of you as lightworkers and servants to implement the balance and harmony of love and wisdom in close association, not as comrades but as friends, with those who would bear arms. Organize them in such a way as to not harm one another. Do you understand?

Response: "Yes, somewhat. I've thought about that quite a bit."

Perhaps you and R.D. can be of assistance in this work, for you see, Dear ones, during this transition, this will be the impulse of many. And is this not the one thing which would endanger much of our work? Much education must be disbursed to these strong willed people. It must be done in a kind and higher way. And yes, it must be done. The disbursement of food will be of vast importance and must not be consolidated into the hands of one or two powers. The power to raise and distribute food must remain with the people. Do you understand?

Question: "Is this pretty much going to be on a community basis, in each area?"

Yes, but there are areas which are more productive than others. And during this transition, these areas will serve as a focus of disbursement. Be prepared for fear and havoc in the lower mind. I realize, Dear ones, this is not fear and havoc in your minds but understand your Brother. Be prepared to serve him from the highest principles.

Question: "Lori had a dream last night where she was shown that the government came out with a map similar to ours. Could you tell us about that dream?"

Very well. We are entering into the two-year period of disbursement of this information and you will see within these next two years, many versions of Earth Change Prophecies. Some will be localized, some generalized, some worldwide, even as changes in the cosmos itself. But let us look realistically at what the source is. We will talk about control and the use of free will. You have asked this question of me and so I feel free to dispense this information to you. Yes, the government will make an attempt to dispel many of the fears over Earth Changes. And in a period, at the end of two years, they will appoint a committee to study and to bring this information to the light. However, their information is geological in nature and thus limited. They do not understand certain mathematical principles, particularly in alignment with the second and third shift. However, their map resembles closely many of the changes which will happen. And there will be much fear and chaos for a period of time, however, it is intended to save lives. But do not forget the focus of the I AM America Map. Do you understand?

Response: "Yes, their map will have a specific purpose for their behind-the-scenes activities in directing certain peoples to certain areas."

This is absolutely correct. The cataclysmic predictions which will be shown upon the government studies will instill such fear in the people they will forget their God Source. That's why it is good for us to have our information out as much as possible before that time. And you must document and date this information now and be prepared when their studies are released. May the light of God shine upon your work. May the light shine within your heart. I AM Saint Germain.

44

Every form of life originates in spirit.

Duality
Sananda
Saint Germain
El Morya

We are in Salt Lake City and heading north to home. But there is one final stop—Dan is fascinated by trance channels and has arranged for us to experience another well-known local medium. I must admit that I am intrigued as I am usually the one in trance. The opportunity to be on the other side will be a unique experience for me.

Her style is quite different from mine. Her eyes are closed but it is apparent that the Spiritual Teacher has taken over her entire body. He uses her hands as he gestures, and he strokes her chin with a masculine quality; this, reminiscent of the technique employed by the famous channel JZ Knight and her teacher Ramtha. As stirring as this method can be—and it is compelling—I'm happy that I employ the technique that Saint Germain and the spiritual teachers have taught and fostered. I may not remember everything that has been said after a trance session, but I always have complete control over my faculties and, as I have explained before, I must heighten my consciousness while the Spiritual Teachers lower theirs. This, they explain, is the spiritual law: "Energy for energy."

I'm not saying that one technique is better than another. Afterall, the focus is truly the message. I do think, however, that channeling methods fit an individual's disposition, their unique energy system, and are calibrated to the channel's level of spiritual evolution.

Later that afternoon, I receive another lesson from the three teachers Saint Germain, Sananda, and El Morya. This is a seminal teaching that introduces the system of Galactic Suns and the Galactic Web—a grid created by the consciousness of everything created, including various human life forms such as aliens, animals, plants, and minerals.

They have a table in front of me. Sananda, Saint Germain and El Morya are here. On the table, they have unrolled a scroll. It is a map of solar systems and what they call the Intergalactic Web. Saint Germain is speaking.

You see, Dear ones, life continues and your planet is not exclusive to life forms. The Planet Earth, or Terra, is at the brink of this understanding and we would be glad to share this information with you. You are in the galaxy which you call the Milky Way, yet to actually understand the galaxy, we would like to discuss the concepts of duality and that of mirroring. If you were to look at the petal of a flower, you have the center of the flower and the petals stemming from the center. What do you see on the reverse of one petal across the center to the next? A petal which is formed precisely like the one opposite it. The solar systems and galaxies are not any different. This mirroring is a common concept we find in all things. There is that which could be called the etheric level or interdimensional level of these solar systems. But first, let's understand the planets and life as you perceive it in the physical. As your planets are laid out and revolve around your central sun, you must understand that your sun is one of twelve within this same Galactic Deity. Do you have any questions?

Question: "You're saying the energy of one Deity is within twelve suns?"

That is correct and contained within the Sun Deity are all universal principles, primarily in terms of structure and duality. You have revolving around your sun, many planets, nine of which you know of, but there are truly twelve. The concept mathematically is twelve times twelve. Do you have any questions?

Question: "What do you mean when you talk of duality? Is that just the positive and the negative?"

Each planet within a given system has its Divine Compliment. Much as you understand the concept of soul clusters and that of twin flames, it is the Divine splitting of consciousness. And while this may appear to take on the form of a physical planet, it is indeed that of consciousness.

Question: "When you refer to the aliens who have caught the attention of the government, are they from a planet which is the duality of this one?"

They are not of this planet's duality. However, duality is a concept which is easily misunderstood. There is also dimensional vibration and they are of a race soon to move and come in to a higher or different vibration.

Question: "I would assume that when Earth makes its change, they would not be able to be within this planet because of the difference in vibration?"

There is a chance they will be here. However, their influence will not be felt by you. They are moving from a Second Dimensional consciousness to Third Dimensional consciousness. You must understand, we deal in physical law and also in laws of consciousness. Your abilities, when you move from Third to Fourth Dimensional consciousness, will allow you to inhabit planets you had never thought possible. And how is this done? Through travel, the traveling of your consciousness, and the command of physical elements. These aliens you speak of are a life force evolving. However, their systems are much simpler. Their mental abilities are fully developed but they have yet to realize the God Source, for this is an evolutionary step. Even the animals upon your planet are more highly evolved in recognition of God Source than these beings. Do you have any questions?

Question: "So they do not have any understanding of the transition we are about to go through?"

They are pulled to your planet through their search for this inner meaning. They have begun to feel the stirrings within their systems of the development of the Heart Center. This has been disruptive to their physical body and yet, they are driven to understand it. We are talking about acceptance.

Question: "Is that what their studies are about, trying to understand the part of us that they lack and have not developed?"

Partially, for their emphasis is on the physical and they have yet to recognize the Third Dimension. However, there are several who are beginning to awake.

Question: "The one who is coming through the channel in southeast Washington, is he of the duality?"

You must understand that many people seek embodiment to learn many things. The one coming through this channel is a split consciousness. Its original embodiment had been upon this planet and yearns to return and so this being seeks a portal of consciousness to travel to this realm to enhance its conscious thoughts.

Through its channeled speaking, it raises its vibration and conscious thought to the development of the Heart Center.

Please understand, all life originates from the spiritual realm of consciousness and densifies to the physical level. And universal principles are the same wherever you go. There is a saying that people are the same wherever you go. The saying here is, universal principle is omnipotent, universal principles apply wherever you go. Terra, Earth, is a planet of the heart. The heart is indeed the Third Dimension and as you begin to evolve to this next dimension, which is that of inner sight, inner vision and that of the intuitive, this cannot occur without having implanted within you that of the heart. Do you understand?

Question: "Yes. What is the purpose of the implants that the aliens have been doing?"

The implants are used as a false third eye, a mechanical third eye, which can be used without the development of the Heart Center that I speak of. This is an implant they have specifically devised for themselves but prefer to test it upon those who have existing Heart Centers. These beings are driven and while it may appear they are driven by a force that is not compatible with the same force you feel directed and driven by, it will be utilized as the same. But we must warn you and give you instruction for the noninterference of your development, for these are universal principles this race has not yet understood. The protection of your emotional body is essential, the Blue Flame of protection and Lord Michael's assistance. You have been given much background material on this work. Do you have questions?

Question: "Lori remembers having a dream of them coming in her house. Was she abducted?"

No, Dear one, the dream was given to her to prepare her to understand this influence. She also had several embodiments where she witnessed invasions from other galaxies. Was it not shortly after that dream that we began our work together? Again, you must understand the forces that work the dualities that we speak of. We have on this table, the map of other galaxies and would like you to understand the nature of what is occurring. For as your planet is ready to engage into the Fourth Dimension, there is another planet ready to engage upon the Third and beyond that another ready to engage to the Second. As thus, they are invaded by that of the Second. Those who move to the Third, and in your case those to the Fourth, seek to understand this, again, as a natural process.

Understand universal principle, for this is indeed the movement of the Third to the Fourth and while you may wonder of the beings who come from the other planets and other dimensional consciousness, keep your light upon that of which you are doing. Keep your light and hold your focus on that which is your work in this conscious realm. As things are presented and situations are presented in your life path, remember we are here to assist you and to help you.

45

Sometimes we do not know that, indeed, "we know."

Harmony

We returned late last night and the first thing I did the next morning was take my bike out for a ride along the beautiful Snake River. The wind was cold and stinging. Winter has arrived and Christmas is quickly approaching. Thankfully, later in the day we are welcomed home by this sweet, yet simple lesson on harmony and self-knowledge.

I AM with you, I AM Saint Germain. Come, I have something to show you.

We are walking through a doorway into a beautiful garden and then beyond this to a gate. He's holding up a key to unlock the gate.

Question: "What is the key for?"

The key to the soul is harmony and peace.

We're passing by a band that's playing.

As you listen to the stringed instruments, do you not hear that each string is in accord with one another? They mix and intermix in a harmonious way, finding themselves to blend with one another. The pathway to harmony is understanding each of the strings and to have them work in a cohesive way together. Peace is something that we strive for and yet, we refuse to see our self as the string that must blend and work with the others. For while you are a part of the whole piece of the music that is being played, you are also the string. The way you wrap yourself around the instrument, tone yourself, and allow yourself to be played by the great hand that is placed upon the instrument is your choice. Remember this the next time you listen to a piece which has been composed, for look at the meaning, the inner meaning of composition. It is not something that has happened in an immediate way. It has been the constructive cooperation among the many to produce the piece. And from this comes the concept of harmony and from this a sense of peace.

Now we're walking on past this band and sitting down at a table. There's a cup in front of me. I'm looking into it.

Look deep within the cup. As you look inside, do you see yourself? Do you see a swirling of feelings, emotions, and thoughts, of which you have no idea what part they play? Remember, while in physical embodiment, this is the challenge, to be responsible for the energy you dispense. You draw these energies back to you like the swirling cup. As you see the water swirl within the goblet, is this not the life force which you too carry? The secret is to not let the droplets fall out of the swirling up. Now, being responsible for containing the swirling living waters within this Cup, when the water edges to the sides, ready to brim over and fall over the edge of the glass, do you not see it is time to calm this water? Now look deeper within this Cup. This vessel holds the light, your light. When I speak to you this way, it is easier for you to understand the concepts that I will introduce to you, for Dear ones, as you are in this physical, is it not easier for you to relate to that which you can touch or see? You are here and now, so I use these ways to describe unseen worlds, unseen concepts. If you have particular questions with the parables I present, please feel free to ask.

Response: "I connected very well to your parables this morning and I can definitely see myself as the string and my challenges being in the here and now."

How tight would you like to be tuned on the instrument? You see, you can allow this for yourself. You have the choice to play the part you would like to play and indeed, it is in the harmony and in conjunction with many others. The use of the will is one of the higher principles we apply to embrace the mind of mankind. For love is the continual power which plays the hearts of man, for it is truly the root of the will and continues to be so. You will see within yourself, as you play your part in the Parable of the Cup, as you learn to contain your energies, there are times you would like to tip the cup and sprinkle the contents over the side. The thrill of the swirling water in the cup is to see the reaction of others and yet, this is learning to contain the waters in the cup. Setting the cup aside, calming the water inside the cup and looking deep into the still contents, there are mysteries which will be revealed to you. I realize I have gone on further than I normally do. If you have your questions, we can continue our instruction for this day.

Question: "What type of work am I doing as I sleep?"

The unconscious activity is a question to man, for it is very difficult for him to be active and to lose the sense of control that he must have over his physical body at all times. As you leave at night, you go for the higher instruction. It is your choice to remember it or not. Remember this, that if you do not recall it immediately, it is because it is your choice. You are being instructed in ways and means which will interact in your life at a given time. After a period of events has occurred, are you frustrated by your ability not to remember or recall?

Response: "I'm frustrated by my lack of perceiving things."

Do not be, for this is your choice. How could you be frustrated by that which you have chosen for yourself? You have chosen it on a more subconscious level.

Response: "I try hard to remember that it is for my own good right now that I am not perceiving things the way I desire to."

Dear chela, remember that you will perceive and you are perceiving. Do you not see the work you are doing? Your Cup swirls enough as it is. Are you to add more ocean to it? You, yourself, have realized this at night. At night, you still the waters in the cup and go within the stilled waters and during the day, again activate the motion within the cup. How much action would you prefer to have? Do you want the water to spill out of the cup? The work you do is indeed for your highest good.

Response: "I don't want the water to spill out of the cup but I guess I assumed that if I had the perceptions, I would be less apt to spill the water. I would have a better understanding."

Since you have asked, I am permitted to give you some details. You go to a planet called Theodra, where you have learned much of structure and its finer use. Your fear of mathematics is well overcome, as you have learned in your inner life. Theodra is a systematic planet, a plane based upon the concepts of accountability and time ratios. You have struggled with these concepts versus matter and are learning, at this inner place, the base relationship of this. Soon you will be equating it in your life.

46

Intention and agreement create our realities.

Agreement
Saint Germain
Sananda

One week after returning home I received a telephone call from Dan's younger sister. "I really need to talk to you," and "Can we meet?" I sensed the urgency in her voice, and we made arrangements to meet for coffee.

Our relationship had always been good—in fact, Jody was very accepting of the spiritual work her brother and I shared. One time when she was having trouble with her daughter, she sought the assistance of Saint Germain, and his words were of great comfort. When I sat down, I intuitively noted that something had changed.

"I hate to tell you this . . ." The look on her face really made me nervous. "When Dan was in Los Angeles he confessed to Susan that he does not see your relationship as permanent." Tears welled up in my eyes and I immediately remembered the cold silence after our immediate departure from Los Angeles prior to the Thanksgiving holiday. Jody reached across the table and touched my hand, "We can't choose who we love, Lori."

I spent several days in an emotional blur. So many thoughts flew in and out of my mind in that period. But I came to the painful conclusion that the spiritual work that Dan and I were both so committed to would never be accepted by his family. Plus, he was under tremendous financial pressure, and our small business was far from solving that problem. In fact, I AM America still needed constant financial support from the funds left over from the sale of my home.

I finally gathered the courage to ask Dan if the conversation was true. He confessed that he loved me, and wanted me to stay, but he was unsure if our relationship would last. He didn't think there would ever be enough money to support the two of us. We came to the amiable agreement that I would run I AM America and that he would return to his advertising business. I decided it was best to move out.

I spent the holidays and the next four weeks at my parents' ranch. It was a comfort to be there, and a stark contrast from our exhilarating trip just weeks ago. My parents offered their empty RV as a short-term office for rolling and mailing Maps. In spite of the chaos and temporary dysfunction that surrounded me, orders for the Map were rolling in. I was even receiving business calls at my parents' telephone number from bookstores throughout the United States ordering dozens of Maps at a time!

The tour had been a success, and the grassroots underground of the alternative spiritual and metaphysical community was abuzz with talk of the Map. I was receiving orders and letters from everywhere in the United States. Yet I deeply missed my friend and partner. After Christmas, I received a letter from Dan; he wrote to let me know that he had finally found the box of towels that we misplaced after the move. At the end of his note he reminded me, "Nothing is lost or wasted! Remember, you are helping so many. . ."

In January a friend hinted that I should move to Coeur d'Alene. She thought that a change of place would do me good and offered to exchange help with marketing and promoting the Map for my assistance with her design and copy on several advertising projects. One night as I moved tubes of Maps from the RV to my car to deliver to the post office in the morning, I looked up at the stars in the cold winter sky. "Please, show me what you want!" I asked the Spiritual Teachers. The next week I rented an apartment in Coeur d'Alene.

As it turned out, my friend who convinced me to move was always busy, and not available, so I was on my own. I had never been so lonely. Some days I would plan a trip to Denny's—to sit and have breakfast in the midday. This was my main social activity of the day! Yet in meditation and dreamtime, my spiritual life was completely dynamic. Inside I felt a recalibration of my spirit, and with time, I grew strong and assured in my daily routine of rolling and mailing Maps.

One day the phone rang. It was Dan. He was planning a business trip to the area and wondered if he could stop by. My heart leaped, "Of course!"

When I opened the door and saw him, I hugged him until my chest hurt! We talked for hours—sorting through business and our relationship. But more importantly, here was my friend—my spiritual companion—and that deep connection to Saint Germain, El Morya, Sananda, Kuthumi, was something that I shared with no one else.

That day turned into a magical week, and we purchased tapes and a new tape recorder and once again the voices of our beloved Spiritual Teachers resonated in the little two-bedroom townhome. More importantly, their spiritual presence and wisdom reverberated in our souls, and we recommitted to their service.

The selection that follows is a lesson on agreement, which mirrors our personal actions and motivations. Obviously, if we were going to work together again, they wanted the two of us to have clarity and transparency.

Understand the accountability of actions, for you can only attract to yourself that which you have brought to your being through self. This will be the greatest teaching to the people at this time, acceptance of the responsibility for the location where they are. For you attract to yourself that which you have brought previously to your being, that which would indicate what needs to be spun off, spun away, as you would call it, from the source of the soul.

Perhaps a person is tempted to steal and what better way for them to take this quality from their lower self but to be in the position where they may be allowed to do so. Perhaps a person has been tempted to murder. They will be placed in the situation where they will be given an opportunity to do so. Do you not see, Dear ones, this is the choice we make? We are learning the responsibility of our own energy. But through the call to the higher Christ Self, the Beloved Mighty I AM Presence, you can take the eternal protection of Blue White Flame, for it was Archangel Michael who came to bind and bound the foreign entities. They have been taken from your Earth Planet and Plane at this time, so the entities that you encounter are those which have been created through the thought form of mankind.

This is the true human experience, the perceptions of good and evil, also with its eternal love. The experiment in the next ten years is to show mankind the eternal truths, the truths which will never leave the face of the planet ever again, for as the vibration moves up into the higher fourth state, mankind will experience the constants. Let me outline these for you please:

1) The Law of Love
2) The Law of Mercy and Forgiveness
3) The Activity of Cosmic Principles

Let me explain this third principle, as the first two principals are comprised in the third concept. One must understand that Earth is not exclusive in its contract and agreement with the universe. There are many other planets which have entered into the same contract and agreement. And you will see, Dear ones, as you experience the third to fourth reality on the Earth Plane and Planet at this time, you will see that throughout the universe, the other planets observe these three laws. They too have been built upon the same laws. Earth is not exclusive in its suffering, for many of the planets have suffered as she has too. And they have felt Divine Compassion toward the Earth Plane and Planet at this time.

To deepen your understanding, perhaps the planet which suffered even greater tests was that of Mars. For you see, the masculine qualities of the planet Mars allowed for horrendous crimes, not only to that of the physical body but to that of the spiritual. Its inhabitants had developed ways to actually enter into the spiritual body and continue the combat. But this was shifted through the recognition of the Divine Vibration of Love, as this universal principle remains throughout the universe.

You must understand the difference between love being an emotion and love as an energy. It is the energy of which all is comprised. And what is the opposite of this energy? The energy of fear and doubt, that which you have known from early Christian theologians as the lack of faith. For love is the ability of the individual to trust. This is the vibration we continue to work with as we develop our bonds of trust with you and give our eternal assistance and support, for this is the next lesson that mankind will learn, the ability to assist and support one another. What are they learning but the energy Vibration of Love? Yes, perhaps this does seem to be a simple explanation and yes, indeed, it is harder to act upon.

These are the eternal truths which you must practice. I've talked much about these principles and now would like to address the principle of the Violet Flame. The Violet Flame is the practicum through which you may come to understand the eternal energy of love. For through the use of the bonding of this energy with yours, you learn Divine Acceptance of the self for what self is. You do not experience the turmoil to the same degree if you are using the Violet Flame.

What a great work this has been for the Planetary Commission to bring the dispensation of the Violet Flame to mankind, for extending Mercy, Forgiveness,

Divine Compassion, and Grace. For you to experience this within your world, you extend this to others. The Violet Flame is not an exclusive contract made between you and the Higher Self. It is a contract which is made and also extended to those about you. As you carry this flame about your body, its ability to transcend all problems is extended to others.

Dear ones, with the use of the Violet Flame, remember there are the universal principles and laws of the three times three. As you enter into the contract of using the Violet Flame, it touches the lives and extends into the hearts of others. This happens not only through oral communication, but perhaps you will be walking and feel the Violet Flame's transcending and uplifting energy extending to those about you. They will look at you and exclaim, "What is this about this person?" It is the Violet Flame! It is the use of the Law of Mercy.

And so you see, Dear ones, through the use of this eternal law, you are able to extend this on to others. We are talking again of a concept you have been exposed to as synergy, the combined energy and effort of the mass. This is truly what we need to have to bring Earth into its evolution. Earth is prepared to move from the Green Ray into the Violet Ray. And how can this happen? Through the assistance of her inhabitants, those who have become part of her and are her. Are not your bodies composed of the earth element itself? And so you must extend the Violet Flame to her, for this is the dispensation of how the Violet Flame is to come to the Earth Planet, through the God beings who inhabit her surface. And now I open the floor for questions.

Question: "What are our tasks now, and what is the priority of these tasks?"

Yes, we have work for you to do. As we have always said, there is much to do to continue your work within the light. But we have stressed the Law of Commitment. Stand firm in where you make your choice. There is much work to be completed and we applaud and commend you for that which you have achieved. It has been a monumental task to step as far as you have stepped, to leave that which you feel as conventional and raise your vibration to our level to extend this to mankind. We applaud you and thank you for the tremendous effort and work. We will continue to dispense the work as you ask to do this. For you see, we are not allowed to infringe upon the free will.

To learn to be responsible for your energies is to understand the power of the Beloved Mighty I AM working within your life. Perhaps you do not understand how strong this power is within you. It is a tremendous force, a force which works on the Law of Attraction.

He is now drawing a diagram on the board.

Commitment = Agreement = Choice/Responsibility = Action = Life Force

As you see this chart Dear ones, do you not understand that all of your actions come with the original agreement and original commitment that you have made? Perhaps this will clarify:

Personal Actions = True Motivations (Life Force)

This is truly magnificent, for you see, this is the way we have interacted with you! We are not allowed to enter into your consciousness for your upliftment without the action of your choice, without the motivation of your pure heart.

Response: "I've been very aware of how my motivations or intent have changed."

This is good, for your ability to recognize this is your ability to carry on the contract with us. For who are we? We extend into the people in your lives. We are not allowed to come into the physical during this transitional time but our work is being carried out by those we call our messengers. And no, we have not set them in the position to be glorified as such, but you must come to the realization that all those within your life are truly messengers, for our energies are subtle and work with all. As you keep your contract and agreement with those about you, it is important that you understand this art, that this is the true way that we function and communicate.

We have formed agreements with you to even speak to you. An agreement is made through the Higher Self. When you dream at night and we bring the visions to you, they are only brought to you through your agreement, through your choice to have the experience. All this is through the responsibility and choice which is yours.

The great Alpha and Omega did not create this energy for you to rely and depend on so strongly. This was not the original intent. The original intent was for the energy to be like that of the parent and to take on typical qualities inherent in the parent. And so the energy must learn to be responsible unto itself. In the same way, the bird is hatched from the egg and nurtured and loved and cared for within the nest and is pushed out to fly and what does it do? In the springtime, it nests again, like that of the parent.

Nature has been brought to you to give you these supreme examples of universal principle. It is by no mistake and design that she is there for you to observe. She brings to the simplest levels, the true lessons. This is the true work of our Elemental Life Force, to bring universal principle to the physical level for man to observe and to watch. For you have been shoved from your nest and must learn to accept the responsibility of your energy, the energy which is like that of the parent. We would like to take a break at this moment to allow you to contemplate these principles.

Music is playing very softly, like birds singing.

We bring the music to you. This is the music of the planet. The violins of the world play for you and what is this but the Elemental Life Force of which we speak. As these birds sing and the winds blow and the sun beats upon your heart, this is the symphony of cooperation and where has this cooperation come from but through agreement. And now beloved Sananda will speak.

Yes, I come to the planet to beg of you to continue this work. I come to you to offer the cup again, to drink and sup with me. For remember me in the Last Supper, when I broke bread with my Brothers and Sisters. This is what we beg of you to do, to break this bread, this lightwork, which you call it. Share and extend this to your Brothers. There are many ways you may do this, to extend that which you know of healing to one another. For understand that you are truly never separated from the Source, but you are feeling your wings from being pushed from the nest. Find your Brothers and Sisters and sup with them. The twelve years of transition have begun and we have called to you to arm yourself with principles of pure salvation. I have said to you, I and the Father are ONE and this I truly mean and that you and I are ONE. You and your Brother, you and your Sister, are truly ONE. Recognize and sup with your family.

Saint Germain takes the floor.

I say to you, Dear ones, call to the Violet Flame. Call to the heart. And I ask you to love and to bless one another and extend this flame from my heart to you, to others. I AM Saint Germain.

47

Love is emotion, energy, and heart.
Let your heart be your guide.

The Safe Harbor

Saint Germain
Sananda
Kuan Yin

When we offered to be of service yet again to the Spiritual Teachers, we had no idea that there would be another Map. Now we have been working on the Earth Changes Map that includes information for Mexico and Central and South America. Saint Germain refers to this Map as the true "I AM America Map," and it will also include information for Canada, which is not yet disclosed.

Dan has followed the same protocol as before, and we purchased several laminated Maps to sketch the information, plus a large World Atlas for reference. The information is copious, but it flows readily and evenly and is a much easier experience than my early days of trance work. So far, we have had about a dozen sessions, and Dan has been traveling up to Coeur d'Alene from Lewiston about every other week. He stays for three to four days and then returns home. In this short amount of time, we are able to get a lot accomplished.

We have decided that all of the transcripts will be organized into a book about the I AM Teachings and the Earth Changes. Dan is still hand-transcribing some recorded sessions and then I enter this information into my word processor, in anticipation of publishing the book. We know that we will publish a larger new version of the I AM America Map—or a World Map—if the Spiritual Teachers give us that material.

During one of his visits, Dan insists that we visit another channel in a public session in Spokane. I feel some resistance, as I know we have so much work to complete, but I know that experiencing direct channeling is his passion. Afterwards, I have an uneasy feeling that I can't pinpoint or identify. I know that change is coming . . . is it an Earth Change?

The next day in trance session we receive the lesson, "The Safe Harbor." Saint Germain, Sananda, and Kuan Yin all reiterate that in matters of love, you must let your heart be your guide.

~

The previous embodiments of the Masters create a pattern of safety you can access. I AM Saint Germain and I stand firm in my commitment to mankind. I say to you, my commitment is strong. Would I release myself from what I have committed to do? I say "no." I AM here.

Question: "Why would a particular channel put out the message that communications where stopped in 1980?"

My Dear ones, there are many who access us. We do not limit ourselves to only those of the holy. Our work is indeed with many and sometimes our words trickle into the minds of smaller men but our words trickle as well into the minds of greater men. Do we stop the flow of the water for one piece of grass? The water flows. Send that message.

Sananda steps forward.

I come to you in love and appreciation of your work and send this message to you. Follow your heart at all times. Follow your heart, for the work that you do is indeed an extension of yourself. There are times we speak of the mind, through which the will functions. And then there is the broader based will, that which is the will of cosmic service. Follow your hearts, Dear ones, to achieve the most appropriate benefit from this work. Be led and guided by your heart. We have spoken of love as energy, other than emotion, and so you have experienced the energy. It is now time to use this energy in all that you do. Listen, look, and receive.

I have come to offer you my support and beg of you to call to me in matters of understanding love, for this is an energy which must continue to flow. It is on the wavelength of this energy that we perform our work with you. It is important to keep this flowing. Yes, this is a form of cooperation but it is the synthesis or end result, as you call it, of cooperation. It is love. We have repeatedly said that all is love and we are most happy to serve you through this. It is our hope that you experience it in greater measure in your life at all times. Do not hesitate to call to us. See us as a safe harbor, for our time in the physical was spent with purpose. Follow your heart,

Dear ones and you are released to universal Oneness.

He is stepping back and Saint Germain is coming forward.

It is with expedient measure, my Dear ones, that I introduce to you Beloved Kuan Yin.

I greet you with the compassion of my heart and being and release this message to mankind:

> The winds begin to blow. The Four Pillars are to shake.
> The seed has been sown. Then the vase is to break.

Question: "What does this mean? The vase is to break? This is the second time we've had reference to the wind coming very soon. Could you be more specific on the event?"

My Dear ones, I am not allowed to give you a date but I am allowed to warn you. It was more a description of the event than the date. I have spoken to you in a form that I am allowed to speak. You see, Dear ones, there are some measures to be taken but I am not allowed to tell you more. Energy, wind, and rain, then, wind and rain. Perhaps we should refer to the Earth Plane in reference to the prose I've given you. It's time to collect yourselves and find a place of meeting. We will continue our work but I send this message of gathering together. My Dear ones, take light of the message. While it is brought in sternness, it is brought for your upliftment. Know you are ONE with us and we are with you.

48

*Communication is a form of energy
that is subtle, yet organized.*

Ley Lines
Saint Germain
Soltec

This is an interesting lesson on ley lines, which are literally ethereal lines of energy that exist among geographical places, ancient monuments, and megaliths. This type of energy is often detected by psychics and mediums, and contains electrical or magnetic points. Golden City Vortices contain several major and many minor ley lines, and this is seminal to understanding their physical and spiritual purpose in the New Times.

⤳

[Editor's Note: This is an excerpt from a technology session regarding the Archtometer. This information is included, as it contains important information on telepathy and ley lines.]

Saint Germain is here with Soltec.

We realize that you have started this with Mafu, who has worked specifically on the harmony and balances. Soltec is here to work with you on the use of communication, also that of the finer energies which will be dispensed.

He's stepping back and Soltec is sitting down at the table. I'm handing him the gyroscope.

Your radius function is a bit distorted but I would like you to understand the energy fields of the spinning of the balls. As was stated last night, there are many, many uses for this device. We are concerned primarily with that of the communication process, for not only is it designed to open up the telepathic portals, it is also designed to work with the lei-line grid. There are clear calculations and mathematical functions in relation to these grids and opening them up clearly for communication. The communication will be brought, not only in that which you feel intuitively but telepathically, the way Earth itself communicates with us. Where do we send our energies? Into the grid. The subtle energies of which we speak form a net that is being woven. Let me explain this further.

Throughout your day, you are aware of the many sources and ways you communicate. You communicate through speech, touch, and eye contact. Though your energies project themselves into many forms of communication, you do not realize the many forms you are unaware of, that are sent out to the universe. There are many forms of communication sent to the Earth Planet and to the subtle level of the web. This is a device through which you break into the web mathematically. This will form an energy field through which one may speak clearly and be heard clearly. There is also a technique that could be used to create the field for those who wish to communicate telepathically.

Response: "Master Chow had mentioned the positive/negative parallel ley lines and that we could bring them together through thought."

There are three layers of ley lines, three layers to be penetrated. This is the intersecting points on the grid, which we will use this device to find. For it is through these intersecting points, portals as you call them, that we are able to penetrate to the third layer. As you penetrate to the third layer up to the portal, you must understand how to travel along these and how the energy is dispensed back down through these portals.

Mafu, whom you have worked with, is the entity assigned with bringing the technical information of harmonizing Earth energy, that of the lower energies, the more primal base energies. I, Soltec, have been assigned to help you with the higher subtle levels of communication and bringing the mathematical calculations into play. Remember, we speak of twelve times twelve and 144. And since we are dealing with energy that is triadic in nature, there are three levels. We are dealing with a base number of four and so, the inner ring is set up on the four. We're speaking of binary numbers.

I believe I have given you enough information for this day. But I will continue to work on this model you have presented to me, making the finer adjustments to it and communicating the information to you. And I turn the floor back to Saint Germain.

Beloved chelas, I would still like to instruct you on the use of the Violet Flame, for you to keep it in your daily meditations. It is of high essential nature, for not only is this the healing of your physical body itself, it is the healing of the layers and opens up the Third Eye. At times, I know I am appearing like a hammering teacher but that is what I AM. I'm here lovingly for your freedom and will continue to work for such. Do you have additional questions?

Response: "No. We're aware we need the hammering."

49

Secrets are revealed in their own time, when one is ready. Do not underestimate hard work and the constant application of your spiritual practice.

Time Projection
Saint Germain
Sananda

We are almost complete with our Earth Changes sessions for South America. This lesson came at the end of a three-day work session of calculating new coastlines and islands. This instruction contains interesting theories on time travel and vital information for the "step-down" of the Masters' presence for healing. This includes both visualization and decrees for the "conscious radiance" of the Spiritual Teacher.

Welcome, Initiates. You have now come to a level of Mastery, Adeptship.

I am apologizing to Saint Germain that we do not have much work planned.

That is okay, for we have work planned for you. We have given you information in your inner visions at night and through traveling to conferences and seminars. These are visions and portals into the future, so that you will have the insights and be willing and ready to act upon them. For you see Dear ones, time travel is there to use for constructive use and yet, if we were to let the barriers down for this to be the common knowledge of the common man, it is a dangerous tool. For yes, this was part of the technology we were asked to impart to the United States government but which we felt could only be imparted to those who were ready to receive it.

The concept of time travel subjectively, is not that which you may give openly and freely, for there entails great responsibility in projecting to the future. You may understand traveling objectively into the past but as you travel to the future, it is that of an interacting quality. When traveling within the past, you gather energies of the emotional body. This is the momentum of duality, for you are objective and yet have used the energy projected from your emotional body. But into the future, you use your subjective mode of thinking and you are allowed personal interactions. It is subjective over objective, whereas traveling to the past is objective over subjective. This is a simple way to understand the concept of responsible time travel. For within the past, there is no interference allowed whatsoever. You go to observe. To the future, you go to submit and to be part.

You are allowed the interaction in your dream state for a specific reason to use in the present. It is an awakening tool for you to understand action versus reaction. The past is primarily comprises reactionary forces. The future comprised of actionary forces. And so, as you synthesize these events to the present day, you are able to make responsible choices, centering and grounding yourself into the present moment. Do you have questions?

Response: "This makes a great tool for governing bodies."

Correct. You, as a group, may travel subjectively into future activities, where you carry your work out on an actionary scale, drawing upon the knowledge of the events of what can happen and yes, in some instances what will happen. When you proceed to travel to the past, you will get what has happened and what cannot be changed. This is where you draw the bulk of your lessons from. However, projecting to the future is another way to bring more lessons and make them fuller within your life presently, for you are able to see the actions of that day and how they do react with that of the next. So, as you look at the past, present, future, do you not see the Divine Thread that runs through all of it? Do you not see how they are all integrated together?

As you travel at night into the future and you come back from the dream state to your waking state, do you not see how the present, as you reflect upon the dream state where you have gone to the future, has instantly become your past? This is the concept of timelessness. Learning to project without the barrier but understanding the rules and principles of interference, you are allowed to go. I will now turn the floor over to Beloved Sananda.

Welcome, Dear ones, as we work on the Initiation of the Heart and understanding its ability to accept and also, at times, reject the eternal truths, we must look at the concept of true healing. This comes from the heart's ability to accept that which is true. Beloved Saint Germain breaks this down for you to understand through many scientific and linear concepts as they relate to healing. I would like to bring this information to you in another way.

Perhaps at times, you find my information tiring and at times, you find my information too simple. But you see, keeping it simple, on a grass roots level, as you call it, allows many to understand and comprehend concepts. And if we need to go to a level of higher understanding and awareness, we shall assist you in further instruction. We have given you ample visualizations and meditations which you can draw upon, but we are particularly concerned with the concept of step-down energetics and the sharing of this conscious activity for that which you call healing. You see, today people feel in their hearts the human condition of separation, the sense of being separated from their Source. This has long been discussed among you. We would like to develop the techniques to allow the splitting of our consciousness to share this consciousness with those who can lay the hands on in the form of healing. For truly, this is the work of the Heart Chakra, the work that comes over the Green and Pink Rays.

I would like to give you a diagram of specific visualizations for allowing our conscious radiance to be shared with yours for the use of tonal and therapeutic healing. Visualizations have been given for the cleansing of the Heart Chakra. It is essential that this be done previous to merging the energies of the Higher Self with an Ascended Being.

Then, call to your Mighty I AM Presence:

> Beloved Mighty I AM, I call to you this moment for the
> shared consciousness of the Ascended Master Sananda
> (or Jesus). I call to his radiance and brilliance to be shared
> with the radiance and brilliance of my I AM Presence.

As they are shared, visualize, Dear ones, how to become ONE, merging first at the level of the I AM, the Higher Self. As the consciousness is merged together, see them taking each other by the hands and embracing one another. Then, hands over their hearts, they direct their energies down, becoming ONE Divine Energy which radiates through the top of the head. The energies pulsate through the Crown Chakra, past the Third Eye and Throat Chakras, and form a large ball of energy within the Heart Chakra.

See a great flame in the heart, coming down from the top of the head, expanding and see its energies charging through your arms. Its resonance will be felt on the palms of your hands. While I have explained this in such a simple and elementary manner, it is essential that you understand the technique. It is through the loving Heart Chakra and the merging of the I AM Presence that this occurs. Do you have any questions?

Question: "I don't remember my dreams or see this energy. I do practice these techniques though. Do you have insights?"

Dear heart, your dreams are that of the inner instruction. Remember, your dreams are also given to you for peaceful awareness, for as you work hard throughout the day, there are times that you need to go into the inner sleep. Perhaps you do not have the ready recall that others do. This should not concern you, for you are very active during the day. And yes, if you will continue your path of practicing and patterning, you will be taking the essential step, for clearly the human must apply in order to learn. Is not this the way you have worked in your many schools with your children? Practice makes perfect.

Question: "Should we share this lesson, this technique with others?"

All of the information we give is meant to share unless stated otherwise. In the next two years, we will be giving information out clearly and openly as an important function of our role here working to assist the planet. For you see, many have spoken of the concept of time speeding up but what we truly have is the speeding up of light. As Saint Germain has spoken to you about the concepts of time and traveling, there clearly is no such thing as time. But the speeding up of light produces an acceleration upon the human and the human perceives this as having less and less time. Actually, what we are getting is more and more time, so that the human becomes more present oriented and expands their energies into the dimension of the Higher Self. So, Dear ones, realize that in the next two years, as we speak through many with much information, as we have many to reach, unless we state, you may share. I AM Sananda, lovingly yours.

50

*Contemplate, meditate, and call to the God-self—this clears
scattered thoughts and cleanses your soul.*

Use of Collective Energy
Saint Germain
Sananda
Kuan Yin
El Morya

When you have doubts or need to make important decisions, it is important to still the inner-self. This is a lesson on contemplation and meditation to clear core issues and to heal the energy system. The Spiritual Teachers counsel, "This is of great benefit and refreshing to the soul."

Saint Germain, Sananda, Kuan Yin, and El Morya are present and we are asking where Kuthumi is, saying that we haven't worked with him lately. They told us that Beloved Kuan Yin has been standing in, in his place, for their work is of the same nature. She is expressing a more feminine side of his work. Saint Germain is introducing Kuan Yin, who would like to speak.

My mission is that of the Dove of Peace. There is much information on stilling the inner self. And why is so much information dispensed and why do we continue to impress it upon your minds? Contemplation is reflection of the soul's energy, that which has occurred and that which must be collected into one directive force. In contemplation, you closely examine the nature of all your actions. When it is said "be still," it is a time of reflection. As you look into the lake, which has stilled its waters, the lake is glassed over. The currents and ripples have stopped. It is a time to observe what is around the lake. You observe the beaches, the reeds, and the waters themselves. Look within them, to the mud at the bottom and the content of the water. In physical embodiment, man must still his energies, for he has many that are directed to many uses. He must still each of them and look at them and see where they fit.

Through this careful examination, you begin to understand. Is this a natural part of the lake or is it simply an object floating on the water which will need to be removed? For, Dear ones, you are attracted and drawn to many energies and there are many energies which are truly not compatible with yours. And so the time to be still, to still the waters, is to see that which floats upon the water. Look at the natural self and understand the purpose of that within your being. Do you have questions?

Question: "Is this why I'm getting so out of balance with the money issues?"

I would like to give this discourse in addressing that issue and also many other issues. It is time to be still in terms of economics. Be still and examine what you need, which is your true nature, which serves as true function and purpose to the true lake. But what comprises the lake again, the structure of the lake? The structure of yourself is what is truly needed.

There is much that has been talked about as structure in the Human Aura and Chakra Systems, however, we prefer to take a much more elemental glance at the issues. We dispense information on energy points and Chakra Systems so you may scientifically understand techniques of visualizations to aid your meditations. These are particularly used for cleansing, clearing, and specifically that of healing. As I address these issues, we must remember, there's such a thing as meditation without visualization. It is the process of becoming calm, of staying in the center balance, so you do not make choices or swim in the water when the wind is blowing. As I have worked with these simple issues and fundamentals of clear meditation, it has allowed the opportunity in my physical embodiments to contemplate the issues at a deeper core level.

What is the need of money? Perhaps there are many needs. We have issues of responsibility and responsibility to what? We have signed agreements of which we have agreed to do. We must still the waters to understand why we have done this. In my embodiments, I have looked clearly for the underlying reasons, the nature of the lake, to why I have allowed the boat to float upon the water. Perhaps you will find within your nature the Divine Attribute. Perhaps you will find that the reason you have allowed the boat to float upon the water is compassion, love. This careful examination of motive is essential. This allows us to be still. Are you prepared to be still and are you prepared to examine closely and to discover your motive?

Response: "I have tried from time to time."

You find it of great benefit and refreshing for your soul. Remember the Divine Principles that you strive to understand: compassion, peace, love, harmony, and cooperation. Perhaps before you go to the place of stillness, write upon a sheet of paper those things, those Divine Attributes which you so much would like to see within your structure, within your lake. You still yourself, look on the many boats which float upon the water and see, do they serve my purpose? Are they part of the attribute I seek? Are they a part of the lake? Dear one, if you have further questions or seek further instruction, I AM glad to assist you.

She's handing a diamond or some sort of a clear stone to me and bowing. Saint Germain begins to speak.

Our Beloved Sister has done much to assist mankind. She has done much to assist mankind in understanding stillness and the benefits acquired from it. Her work has been hard and yet complete. She has given to mankind an understanding of compassion and peace. Beloved El Morya would like to speak again upon the right use of perception.

Dear ones, I come to you from the inner retreat, away from the scattered thoughts which occur within you throughout the day. If you were to list on a sheet of paper the many thoughts which go in and out of yourself throughout the day, you would be busy with the paper itself. Hen scratching upon it, as each thought hammers and each thought boomerangs throughout yourself. Perhaps you have experienced days where it seems as if your body will explode with the energy of thought that is arrowing through it. And what is the cure for this? Directive thought, allowing the thought to go to the central core of that which you are and saying, "is this thought consistent with my directive belief?"

Each day, as you turn your will over to that Mighty Force, that Mighty Force which gives your physical body its life, ask for the directive purpose of the day. Is that day a day of truth? Is that day a day of freedom? Is that day a day for healing? Is that day a day for peace? Is that day a day for contemplation? And as the thoughts are targeted and shot at you, it is your perception of how they relate to the directive force of the day. This too is another exercise that we would like to give to you for learning. We are teaching you to use your energy in a collective manner. You must adjust your perception of how you understand the events in a day.

In the beginning of the day, still yourself and ask your Mighty God-Self to impress to you that which your day is to be, if you are to have a day of discernment. You will be presented that day with many thoughts and experiences from which you will be allowed to choose. The same, as if your Mighty God Source commands to you a day for peace, whichever thought and action which comes to you that day, you will say to yourself, "I AM at peace." Do you understand this exercise that we give to you? You must call each day to your God Source and then use your God Mind. For remember, the life that beats your heart, the source of that energy. This technique, though simple, is important to practice. I AM here for your assistance.

Sananda steps forward.

Perhaps to address these issues more clearly, Dear hearts, we should explain to you that this session the Beloved Saint Germain is facilitating is to understand the use of your collective energies. And I would like to address the issues surrounding the interaction with others. Kuan Yin has clearly addressed the process of being within the self. Beloved El Morya has clearly addressed the issue of being with the mind. I would like to address the issue of being with others, for when you are with others, do you not have the collective mind and the collective self?

I speak in a simple way and that is, love one another. I speak also of the heart. Realize the connection that occurs, not only in a physical geometric pattern. We have explained technicalities to you but now we will speak to you in what you would call layman's terms. For as you interact with one another and seek to have a calming effect, seek to have that for the most constructive use, to continue your work for clearing and cleansing.

I would like to speak to you of collective healing, for even in conversations, do we not heal one another as we speak to each other? For as we have spoken to you many times, it has helped to raise our vibration and as you speak to us, does it not help to raise your vibration? We're speaking of the reciprocal relationship of healing, that which is the two way path. When you ask a favor of a person, realize the reciprocal relationship. When you converse with another, realize again the two-way path.

The word "healing," in your day and age, is much over used and if we were to explain the concept in the most simple fashion, we would give it one word, "merge." For healing is the practice of removing separation. Healing is a process that occurs when one accepts the interaction of another in their path. There are those who have self-healed but how have they done this? Through acceptance of the self: merge. And there are many who go for healing who say, "I have this great disease, remove it for me." And again, what has occurred: merge. We have given you much to think about this day. You may say this is simple but we clearly would like for you to contemplate that which has been given to you. I AM here lovingly for your assistance.

Saint Germain steps forward.

Beloved children of the flame, these good beings have come to you this day to offer to you some of the first building blocks that have assisted them while they were in physical embodiment. And if you ask of me what I would I give you, I would say look within the science of yourself. Look to your nature. See within yourself the qualities that are most like your God Source and use them, for this is what we would explain as talent and ability. Use them to the fullest capabilities, and develop the ones which you may assume you are lacking. But really, there is no such thing as lack. There is only that which has not yet been developed to the full capability.

51

We are learning to become ONE with our energy.

The Christ Plane
Saint Germain
Sananda

Prior to receiving this remarkable instruction, Dan and I sadly admitted to one another that we were over. Apparently our work together was "finished" or, better said, "it was complete." However, this time I knew with certainty that we would both move on with confidence in our spiritual growth and evolution. I was invited to tour again, this time in the Pacific Northwest, with speaking engagements in Spokane, Wenatchee, Seattle, Port Townsend, and Olympia. It might be difficult to present the slideshow and the Map material without him.

Dan found another channel that he wants to work with. Do you remember the lesson, "Safe Harbor?" He decided to follow his heart, and I wouldn't want it any other way.

After my first solo presentation of the Map in Spokane, I walked out to my car and there stood Dan, waiting for me. He walked over and handed me a white feather. "I wanted to tell you good luck, and Happy Birthday." I hugged him, thanked him, and stuck the feather in the sun visor. As I drove off, I turned on the radio and Carly Simon was singing one of the last verses of "Let the River Run." No, it wasn't a happy day for me, but it was a good day. And tomorrow was my birthday—I would be thirty-three years old.

This is my last session with Dan, "The Christ Plane." And this is the last of fifty-one lessons in this book about the I AM Presence—the individualized presence of God. I summarize the words of the Spiritual Teachers, "Welcome your lessons along the path . . . accept the lessons along the path. This is your desire to be whole." So be it.

I'm here in a green room with Saint Germain and Sananda. Saint Germain speaks.

As we work with you on levels of Mastery and as you walk in the physical embodiment, you discover that your experiences become, what you would term, "intense." However, we are talking about the awakening of your soul to that which you seek, resolution. And while there is truly no separation between you and the creative God Force, you work to dissolve that which hampers or impedes you from where you want to be. As you see where you want to be or think where you want to be, you go through a process of walking down this path. In the course of walking on the path you discover, is this truly where I want to be? And as the lessons are presented to you, like little shards of glass as you walk on the path, they embed in your feet and you cry, "this is not the path I wanted to walk upon." You must pick this glass from your feet and remember the teachings and the sound principles of this work. Pick the glass from your feet and stand up and walk, for your feet are truly not bleeding. What you have done is eliminated energy and vibration from yourself that is not needed.

You have spent many embodiments using energy and yes, sometimes using this energy in a way that is not constructive to yourself. However, it is the realization of the use of this energy within yourself that is now constructive to yourself, which works to eliminate embedded energy. As it works itself to the surface, do you not say this is painful? For it is like the shard of glass. But welcome the shard coming to the surface, for you are working towards becoming whole and as this energy leaves your system, your bodies and the many layers of the etheric come to the realization of how good it is that now you know the right use of energy.

Welcome your lessons along the path, chelas. Accept the lessons along the path. And yes truly, to indicate that there is a lesson would indicate that you are not whole. But it is because of your desire to be whole that we continue our work with you. We have given you meditations, visualizations, and proof of our existence and yet, you do not see us. You hear from us only in the many ways which we are now allowed to contact you. For understand, our vibration is such that we are only allowed to contact in a certain way at this present moment. As you raise the frequency and vibration through the elimination of the misuse of energies, you allow a vibration, a resonance around your system, which we find acceptable as a pathway to further our communication with you. For this is truly the process of what you call channeling.

Beyond that, there is another process which goes beyond channeling, that which is the merging of consciousness with your consciousness. Your visual sense merges with our visual sense and our sound and auditory systems merge. There have been times where we have been given the dispensation to appear to you in physical, visible, tangible bodies; however, during the transition, this is not possible. Until you have raised the level of vibration, the resonance of which I speak, then we will lower ours so that we come to this plane that we call the Christ. And how do you find the Christ? Is it going within? Of course, it is going within. And how do you go within to reflect upon the experiences that you have on the outer? Each day, as you travel about interacting with others, you gather among you that which you reflect within, for you are learning to be at ONE with your energy.

While we would like to say "control your energy," we emphasize, it is more clearly being responsible for your energies. How do you react to each situation throughout the day? Do you have questions? As we get into a path and start getting the shards of glass into our feet, is it better just to pull the shards out and continue on that path or to vary the path? The choice is yours of how you travel along the path but the path is the path. Dear one, have you seen a street in the city, a major street which will take you there quickly and along the street there are many stop lights? So, the same process will happen, no matter how much we vary it as we continue to grow.

The same process occurs, whether you turn to the right or the left off of this main street and go around the block a few times, as your saying says. Perhaps going around the block has been a pleasant experience or perhaps, all it has done is kept you off the main path. My reference to shards of glass and pulling them out is exactly that. Pull the shards from your feet and continue your walk. Welcome that you can pull the shards from your feet, that you recognize them, for there was a point in time where you would not even recognize the shard of glass in your foot. This is what I speak of, walking with joy along the path. Laugh at your experiences and see the joy in removing the glass. Do you understand?

Response: "Yes, recognizing what is happening for the higher purpose."

This is a universal principle of realizing that when there is something that needs to be, as you would say "fixed," that this is the process of doing it. You look and say "this is broken" and your conscious recognition of that which is broken allows you to accept, fix, or divert it. But as your path becomes more intense, as we work with you for the higher Initiations and as you ask to do our work, I ask of you to fix. I ask of you to continue my work, as you have asked of me to assist you. It is rare that an Ascended Master infringes upon the free will of a human, that Christ Self embodied in a human body. But one area that we are allowed to infringe, at this moment, is to say to you, "Will you do my work?" For what is this work but clearly the work of the God Source, that of which we are all ONE. And as you ask me for assistance, remember that we will all be there for your assistance, lovingly pouring forth the streams of blessings and love from the heavenly host, that which is your true Home. For as we gather you under our wings, we will continue to bless you and treat you as one of the flock that you are.

"Let the river run,
let all the dreamers wake the nation.
Come, the New Jerusalem.

Silver cities rise,
the morning lights
the streets that lead them,
and sirens call them on
with a song.

It's asking for the taking.
Trembling, shaking.
Oh, my heart is aching.

We're coming to the edge,
running on the water,
coming through the fog,
your sons and daughters.

We the great and small
stand on a star
and blaze a trail of desire
through the dark'ning dawn."

- from "Let the River Run," by Carly Simon

Spiritual Lineage of the Violet Flame

The teachings of the Violet Flame, as taught in the work of I AM America, come through the Goddess of Compassion and Mercy, Kuan Yin. She holds the feminine aspects of the flame, which are Compassion, Mercy, Forgiveness, and Peace. Her work with the Violet Flame is well documented in the history of Ascended Master teachings, and it is said that the altar of the etheric Temple of Mercy holds the flame in a Lotus Cup. She became Saint Germain's teacher of the Sacred Fire in the inner realms, and he carried the masculine aspect of the flame into human activity through Purification, Alchemy, and Transmutation. One of the best means to attract the beneficent activities of the Violet Flame is through the use of decrees and invocation. However, you can meditate on the flame, visualize the flame, and receive its transmuting energies like "the light of a thousand suns," radiant and vibrant as the first day that the Elohim Arcturus and Diana drew it forth from our solar sun at the creation of Earth. Whatever form, each time you use the Violet Flame, these two Master Teachers hold you in the loving arms of its action and power.

The following is an invocation for the Violet Flame to be used at sunrise or sunset. It is utilized while experiencing the visible change of night to day, and day to night. In fact, if you observe the horizon at these times, you will witness light transitioning from pinks to blues, and then a subtle violet strip adorning the sky. We have used this invocation for years in varying scenes and circumstances, overlooking lakes, rivers, mountaintops, deserts, and prairies; in huddled traffic and busy streets; with groups of students or sitting with a friend, but more commonly alone in our home or office, with a glint of soft light streaming from a window. The result is always the same: a calm, centering force of stillness. We call it the Space.

Invocation of the Violet Flame for Sunrise and Sunset

I invoke the Violet Flame to come forth in the name of I AM that I AM,

To the Creative Force of all the realms of all the Universes, the Alpha, the Omega, the Beginning, and the End,

To the Great Cosmic Beings and Torch Bearers of all the realms of all the Universes,

And the Brotherhoods and Sisterhoods of Breath, Sound, and Light, who honor this Violet Flame that comes forth from the Ray of Divine Love—the Pink Ray, and the Ray of Divine Will—the Blue Ray of all Eternal Truths.

I invoke the Violet Flame to come forth in the name of I AM that I AM!

Mighty Violet Flame, stream forth from the Heart of the Central Logos, the Mighty Great Central Sun! Stream in, through, and around me.

(Then insert other prayers and/or decrees for the Violet Flame.)

Glossary

Agreement Formation: The sacred meeting of two minds which on one formative side reflects our intent and commitment. The result of our agreements with others mirrors our choices and our responsible actions which define our life force. Since our actions illustrate our motivations, agreements reflect our ability to effectively Co-create with others, and produce the level of harmony we enjoy from the interaction.

Alpha-Omega: According to Ascended Master teachings, our solar sun is one of seven evolved suns from the lineage of Twelve Ancestral Suns. Alpha and Omega—our current Great Central Sun—is overseen by a larger ancestral sun, known in Ascended Master myth as the Mighty Elohae-Eloha. It is claimed that of the twelve great central suns, Alpha and Omega is the fourth; and from their lineage seven smaller suns evolve: the Seven Galactic Suns. The fourth sun of the Seven Galactic Suns is Helios and Vesta, Earth's sun.

Ancient of Days, also known as Sanat Kumara: Sanat Kumara is a Venusian Ascended Master and the venerated leader of the Ascended Masters, best known as the founder of Shamballa, the first Golden City on Earth. He is also known in the teachings of the Great White Brotherhood as the Lord of the World and is regarded as a savior and eminent spiritual teacher.

Archangels *(the Seven):* The seven principal angels of creation are: Michael, the Blue Ray; Jophiel, the Yellow Ray; Chamuel, the Pink Ray; Gabriel, the White Ray; Raphael, the Green Ray; Uriel, the Ruby Ray; and Zadkiel, the Violet Ray.

Atlantis: An ancient civilization of Earth, whose mythological genesis was the last Puranic Dvapara Yuga—the Bronze Age of the Yugas, and its demise occurred around the year 9628 BC. The legends of Atlantis claim the great empire co-existed with Ameru, Lemuria, and the Lands of Rama. According to Theosophical thought, Atlantis's evolving humanity brought about an evolutionary epoch of the Pink Ray on Earth, and the development of the Astral-Emotional bodies and the Heart Chakra. Ascended Master provenance claims the Els—now the Mighty Elohim of the Seven Rays—were the original Master Teachers to the spiritual seekers of Atlantis. Esoteric historians suggest three phases of political and geophysical boundaries best describe its ancient record: the Toltec Nation of Atlantis (Ameru); the Turian Nation of Atlantis (the invaders of the Land of Rama); and Poseid, the Island Nation of the present-day Atlantic Ocean. The early civilizations of Atlantis were ruled by the spiritually evolved Toltec and their spiritual teachings, ceremonies, and temples were dedicated to the worship of the sun. Atlantean culture later deteriorated into the use of nuclear weapons and cruelty towards other nations, including the use of genetic engineering. The demise of Atlantis was inevitable;

however, modern-day geologists, archaeologists, and occultists all disagree to its factual timing. Ascended Master teachings affirm that Atlantis—a continent whose geophysical and political existence probably spanned well over 100,000 years—experienced several phases of traumatic Earth Change. This same belief is held by occult historians who allege Earth repeatedly cycles through periods of massive Earth Change and cataclysmic pole-shifts that activate tectonic plates which subsequently submerge whole continents and create vital new lands for Earth's successors.

Apex: The center, especially the top of a Golden City Vortex.

Ascended Masters: Once an ordinary human, an Ascended Master has undergone a spiritual transformation over many lifetimes. He or she has Mastered the lower planes—mental, emotional, and physical—to unite with his or her God-Self or I AM Presence. An Ascended Master is freed from the wheel of Karma. He or she moves forward in spiritual evolution beyond this planet; however, an Ascended Master remains attentive to the spiritual well-being of humanity, inspiring and serving the Earth's spiritual growth and evolution.

Ascension: A process of Mastering thoughts, feelings, and actions that balance positive and negative Karmas. It allows entry to a higher state of consciousness and frees a person from the need to reincarnate on the lower earthly planes or lokas of experience. Ascension is the process of spiritual liberation, also known as *moksha*.

Ascension Valley: According to the I AM America Prophecies, Ascended Masters appear in physical form in the Golden City Vortices during and after the twenty-year period. At that time, Mass Ascensions occur in the Golden Cities, at the Star or center locations of these Vortices, and in select locations around the world, which are hosted by the complimentary energies of Mother Earth. A model of this type of location is Ascension Valley located in the Shalahah Vortex.

Blue Ray: A Ray is a perceptible light and sound frequency, and the Blue Ray not only resonates with the color blue, but is identified with the qualities of steadiness, calm, perseverance, transformation, harmony, diligence, determination, austerity, protection, humility, truthfulness, and self-negation. It forms one-third of the Unfed Flame within the heart—the Blue Ray of God Power, which nourishes the spiritual unfoldment of the human into the HU-man (the God-Man). Use of the Violet Flame evokes the Blue Ray into action throughout the light bodies, where the Blue Ray clarifies intentions and assists the alignment of the Will.

Chakra(s): Sanskrit for wheel. Seven spinning wheels of human-bioenergy centers stacked from the base of the spine to top of the head.

Chakra System: The human energy system of the seven chakras, including the Kundalini. In Sanskrit, *Kundalini* literally means coiled, and represents the coiled energy located at the base of the spine, often established in the lower Base and Sacral Chakras. *Kundalini Shatki* (*shatki* means "energy") is claimed to initiate spiritual development, wisdom, knowledge, and enlightenment.

Christ, the, or Christ Consciousness: The highest energy or frequency attainable on Earth. The Christ is a step-down transformer of the I AM energies, which enlighten, heal, and transform all human conditions of degradation and death.

Christ Self: Christ Self, also known as the Higher Self or Guardian Angel, protects the physical body, even though it operates at a lower vibratory rate than the I AM Presence. It also provides an intermediary power between the I AM Presence and the outer human form. Simply speaking, this intelligent body of light serves the energies of the I AM as a Step-down Transformer and a propellant of action in the physical plane.

Circle of the Violet Flame: The use of the Violet Flame, especially for protection, is known as the Circle of the Violet Flame.

Consciousness: Awakening to one's own existence, sensations, and cognitions.

Crown Chakra: Known in Sanskrit as the *Sahasrara*, this chakra is located at the top of or just atop of the head. This Chakra connects our human consciousness to the spiritual planes. The Crown Chakra, also known as the Seventh Chakra is perhaps the most unique of the seven chakras as this is where the Seven Rays enter the Chakra System. In the Hindu system the Crown Chakra is also known as the Chakra of One-Thousand Petals.

Cup: The Ascended Masters often refer to our human body as a cup filled with our thoughts and feelings; it is also a symbol of neutrality and grace.

Descent: The process of the soul entering physical embodiment on Earth.

Deva: Shining one or being of light.

Divine Circle of Completion: The philosophic notion that all creations, great and small, originate from one, organic Source.

Divine Compliment: The idea that the ONE creative spark of the soul's genesis divides into two distinct parts: one part female, the other part male. The twin aspects of the soul play a number of roles with each other throughout successive lifetimes, and as the soul evolves and spiritually grows this interaction perfects and expands. This same concept is known as Twin Flames; however the term Divine Compliment specifically describes the twin aspects of the soul as it exists in the Fifth Dimension, free from the karmic implications of the lower planes and harmonizing through the causal plane of spiritual purity and unconditional love.

Dove: A symbol of universal peace; however, the Ascended Masters teach that the dove is also the symbol of one age transitioning into a new one.

Duality: An understanding that the world is divided into two perceptible categories

Earth Changes: A prophesied Time of Change on Earth, including geophysical, political, and social changes alongside the opportunity for spiritual and personal transformation.

Elemental: A nature-being.

El Morya: Ascended Master of the Blue Ray, associated with the development of the will.

Elohim: Creative beings of love and light that helped manifest the divine idea of our solar system. Seven Elohim (the Seven Rays) exist here. They organize and draw forward Archangels, the Four Elements, Devas, Seraphim, Cherubim, Angels, Nature Guardians, and the Elementals. The Silent Watcher—the Great Mystery—gives them direction.

Emotional Body: A subtle light-body of the Human Aura comprising emotions.

Field *(Light)*: The field of light surrounding the human body; the aura.

Fiery Seed: An atomic cell located in the human heart. It is associated with all aspects of perfection and contains and maintains a visceral connection with the Godhead. The shape is an octagon, with twelve points and thirteen facets.

Feast of Light: An Ascended Master ceremony where members of the Brotherhood meet and celebrate the light within.

Fourth Dimension: A dimension of vibration associated with telepathy, psychic ability, and the dream world. This is the dimension of the Elemental Kingdom and the development of the super-senses.

Four Pillars: The provenance of this spiritual teaching is designed to achieve the Christ Consciousness and comes from an ethereal scroll: *The Truth of Ages*. Here are its tenants, which are four fundamental spiritual teachings: (1) Turn your will over to the Universal Christ and this opens the necessary intuitive knowledge which initiates the self into Selfhood. (2) Thoughts manifest; work to transform judgments towards one another into love. (3) Remember that your spiritual path and Divine Purpose are separate and unique and attained through the ideals of Spiritual Freedom. Wholeheartedly embrace this freedom, and give it to others. (4) Love one another.

Galactic Web: A large galactic grid which encircles Earth. The grid is created by the consciousness of everything throughout the galaxy including various human life-forms, animals, plants, and minerals.

Golden Age: A peaceful time on Earth prophesied to occur after the Time of Change. It is also prophesied that during this age, human life spans are increased and sacred knowledge is revered. During this time, the societies, cultures, and the governments of Earth reflect spiritual enlightenment through worldwide cooperation, compassion, charity, and love. Ascended Master teachings often refer to the Golden Age as the Golden-Crystal Age and the Age of Grace.

Golden City of Klehma: The fifth United States Golden City located primarily in the states of Colorado and Kansas. Its qualities are continuity, balance, and harmony; its Ray force is White; and its Master Teacher is Serapis Bey.

Golden City of Malton: The second United States Golden City located in the states of Illinois and Indiana. Its qualities are fruition and attainment; its Ray force is Gold and Ruby; and its Master Teacher is Kuthumi.

Golden City Vortex: According to the prophecies, these large Vortex areas are havens of safety and spiritual growth during the Time of Change.

Gold(en) Flame: An energy field of spiritual enlightenment. The teachings of the Golden Flame are said to originate from the Pleiades.

Great Purification: Primarily considered a Native American term, the Great Purification signals the end of one period of time for humanity and the beginning of a New Time.

Great White Brotherhood and Sisterhood (Lodge): This fraternity of ascended and unascended men and women is dedicated to the universal uplifting of humanity. Its main objective includes the preservation of the lost spirit, and the teachings of the ancient religions and philosophies of the world. Its Mission: to reawaken the dormant ethical and spiritual spark among the masses. In addition to fulfilling spiritual aims, the Great White Lodge has pledged to protect mankind against the systematic assaults—which inhibit self-knowledge and personal growth—on individual and group freedoms.

Green Ray: The Ray of Active Intelligence is associated with education, thoughtfulness, communication, organization, the intellect, science, objectivity, and discrimination. It is also adaptable, rational, healing, and awakened. The Green Ray is affiliated with the planet Mercury.

Heart Chakra: The location of this chakra is in the center of the chest and is known in Sanskrit as the *Anahata*. Its main aspect is Love and Relationships; our ability to feel compassion, forgiveness, and our own feeling of Divine Purpose.

Higher Self: The *Atma* or *Atman*. This is the true identity of the soul which resides in the spiritual planes of consciousness, and although it is energetically connected to each individual in the physical plane, the Higher Self is free from the Karmas of the Earth Plane and identification with the material world.

I AM America Map: The Ascended Masters' Map of prophesied Earth Changes for the United States.

I AM: The presence of God.

I AM Presence: The individualized presence of God.

Initiation: Admission, especially into secret, advanced spiritual knowledge.

Interdimensional mathematics: A yet-to-be discovered set of scientific principles that explain the existence of the unseen worlds. Much of the phenomenon of the New Times—namely the Golden Cities—is explained through its science.

Kuan Yin: The Bodhisattva of Compassion and teacher of Saint Germain. She is associated with all the Rays and the principle of femininity.

Kuthumi: An Ascended Master of the Pink, Ruby, and Gold Rays. He is a gentle and patient teacher who works closely with the Nature Kingdoms.

Lady Opportunity or Goddess of Opportunity: Also known in Ascended Master teachings as Portia, the Goddess of Justice, Lady Opportunity serves on the Seventh Ray. She is the Divine Compliment of Master Saint Germain and her symbol is the scales of justice. As an embodiment of the energies of Divine Mother, her golden scales symbolize the perfect balance of mercy and justice.

Ley lines: Lines of energy that exist among geographical places, ancient monuments, megaliths, and strategic points. These energy lines contain electrical or magnetic points.

Lemuria: An ancient civilization that existed before Atlantis, largely in the South Pacific North America, Asia, and Australia.

Lightworker: A person devoted to the upliftment of humanity through self-development and spiritual growth. At this time many lightworkers are also members of the Great White Brotherhood and are jointly dedicated to Earth's and humanity's spiritual evolution alongside the worldwide peace and Ascension Process of the New Times.

Lord Meru: An Ascended Master of the Ruby and Gold Ray is also known as the great Sage of Ancient Mu. Lord Meru is a teacher of the ancient civilizations of Earth and considered a spiritual historian of their mythological records.

Love: "Light in action."

Madame Blavatsky: H. P. Blavatsky is considered by many to be the Mother of the New Age. She is the founder of Theosophy and the Theosophical Society.

Mafu: One of twelve spiritual Brothers who is currently working for the spiritual growth and upliftment of humanity and Earth. He is known as the *Master of Harmony*, creating balance with Earth at this important time.

Maltese Cross: A symbol often used by Saint Germain, representing the Eight-Sided Cell of Perfection (the geometric Fiery Seed), and the human virtues of honesty, faith, contrition, humility, justice, mercy, sincerity, and the endurance of persecution.

Master of Oneness: An Ascended Master who assists students to understand and acclimate to the energies of the ONE in the Ascension Process. His symbol is a gold circle.

Master Rada: A messenger of the Pink Ray, Master Rada resides in Tibet.

Mental Body: A subtle light-body of the Human Aura comprising thoughts.

Mudra: A symbolic ceremonial or spiritual gesture, mostly expressed by the hands and fingers. It is often used by evolved spiritual beings and Ascended Masters to signify or emit spiritual energies.

Navel Chakra: Also known as the *Solar Plexus*, this chakra is located between the navel and the base of the sternum. It is an intense feeling (intuitive) chakra which is known as the *Center of Power and Balance* in relationship to everything in life.

New Age: Prophesied by Utopian Francis Bacon, the New Age would herald a United Brotherhood of the Earth. This Brotherhood-Sisterhood would be built as *Solomon's Temple*, supported by the four pillars of history, science, philosophy, and religion. These four teachings would synergize the consciousness of humanity to Universal Fellowship and Peace.

ONE: Indivisible, whole, harmonious Unity.

Oneness: A combination of two or more, which creates the whole

Paul the Venetian: An Ascended Master of the Pink, White, and Green Rays. Paul the Venetian identifies with the qualities of cooperation and beauty through art, architecture, music, and literature.

Pink Ray: The Pink Ray is the energy of the Divine Mother and associated with the moon. It is affiliated with these qualities: loving, nurturing, hopeful, heartfelt, compassionate, considerate, communicative, intuitive, friendly, humane, tolerant, adoring.

Prophecy: A spiritual teaching given simultaneously with a warning. It's designed to change, alter, lessen, or mitigate the prophesied warning. This caveat may be literal or metaphoric; the outcomes of these events are contingent on the choices and the consciousness of those willing to apply the teachings.

Ray: A force containing a purpose, which divides its efforts into two measurable and perceptible powers: light and sound.

Saint Germain: Ascended Master of the Seventh Ray, Saint Germain is known for his work with the Violet Flame of Mercy, Transmutation, Alchemy, and Forgiveness. He is the sponsor of the Americas and the I AM America material. Many other teachers and Masters affiliated with the Great White Brotherhood assist his endeavors.

Sananda: The name used by Master Jesus in his ascended state of consciousness. Sananda means joy and bliss, and his teachings focus on revealing the savior and heavenly kingdom within.

Serapis Bey: An Ascended Master from Venus who works on the White Ray. He is the great disciplinarian—essential for Ascension; and he works closely with all unascended humanity who remain focused for its attainment.

Seven Rays: The traditional Seven Rays of Light and Sound are: the Blue Ray of Truth, the Yellow Ray of Wisdom, the Pink Ray of Love, the White Ray of Purity, the Green Ray of Healing, the Gold and Ruby Ray of Ministration, and the Violet Ray of Transmutation.

Seventh Race or Seventh Manu: Highly evolved lifestreams prophesied to embody on Earth from 1981 to 3650 AD. Their goal is to anchor freedom and the qualities of the Seventh Ray into planetary conscious activity. They are prophesied as the generation of peace and grace for the Golden Age. South America is their forecasted home, though small groups will incarnate in other areas of the globe.

Silver Cord: A cord of life, light, and power which connects the human energy system from the Crown Chakra to the I AM Presence. The Silver Cord is the soul's divine connection from the earthly planes to the astral and spiritual planes of consciousness.

Soltec: An Ascended Master of science and technology who is affiliated with the Green Ray.

Spirit-guide: An Ascended or unascended spiritual teacher who assists souls on their journey of evolution and spiritual growth on Earth. A Spirit Guide resides in the spiritual planes of consciousness.

Theory of the Void: Saint Germain's metaphysical teachings that embrace galactic portals to other dimensions of life experience.

Third-Eye Chakra: Also known as the *Ajna Chakra*, this energy center is located above and between the eyebrows. The Third-eye Chakra blends thought and feeling as perception and projection for Co-creative activity.

Throat Chakra: Located at the throat area, this chakra is also known as *Vishuddha*. It is associated with Expression of truth, emotion, creativity, knowledge, and the sciences.

Time of Change: The period of time currently underway. Tremendous changes in our society, cultures, and politics in tandem with individual and collective spiritual awakenings and transformations will abound. These events occur simultaneously with the possibilities of massive global warming, climate changes, and seismic and volcanic activity—Earth Changes. The Time of Change guides the Earth to a New Time, the Golden Age.

Violet Flame: The Violet Flame is the practice of balancing Karmas of the past through Transmutation, Forgiveness, and Mercy. The result is an opening of the Spiritual Heart and the development of *bhakti*—unconditional love and compassion. It came into existence when the Lords of Venus first transmitted the Violet Flame, also knows as Violet Fire, at the end of Lemuria to clear Earth's etheric and psychic realms, and the lower physical atmosphere of negative forces and energies. This paved the way for the Atlanteans, who used it during religious ceremonies and as a visible marker of temples. The Violet Flame also induces Alchemy. Violet light emits the shortest wavelength and the highest frequency in the spectrum, so it induces a point of transition to the next octave of light.

Violet Ray: The Seventh Ray is primarily associated with Freedom and Ordered Service alongside Transmutation, Alchemy, Mercy, Compassion, and Forgiveness. It is served by the Archangel Zadkiel, the Elohim Arcturus, the Ascended Master Saint Germain, and Goddess Portia.

Vortex: A polarized motion body that creates its own magnetic field, aligning molecular structures with phenomenal accuracy. Vortices are often formed where ley lines (energy meridians of Earth) cross. They are often called power spots as the natural electromagnetic field of Earth is immensely strong in this type of location.

Weather Crystal: An energy anomaly prophesied to exist in the New Times whereby the Cycle of the Elements ceases, and timelessness occurs. The underlying principle of this concept is alleged to exist in the science of crystals, and this technology is prophesied to control the weather in the New Times.

Will: Choice.

Wisdom Ray (Yellow Ray): Associated with the planet Jupiter and also known as the Divine Guru. It is affiliated with expansion, optimism, joy, and spiritual enlightenment.

Zero-Point: A conscious neutral position that exists beyond duality and cultivates the Christ Consciousness.

Appendix A

Fifty-One Lessons: A Review
The I AM Presence

1. Inspiration, Intuition, and the Higher Self. Contact and communication opens with thanks and appreciation. Differences are seen between the Higher Self, an Ascended Master, a Spirit Guide from many lifetimes, and a Nature Spirit for earthly inspiration.

2. Manifestation and Spiritual Development. An energy stream from the center of the right hand with the left hand over the heart, while asking for the Divine Highest Good, is used for manifestation. Imagine yourself as a Vortex.

3. Ancient Technology. A type of gyroscope can predict and measure Earth Changes.

4. Silver Cord. A cord from the Heart Chakra is a portal of communication and the ease of its use is based upon openness.

5. Heaven on Earth. The final polar shift will be more dramatic, as it opens up the etheric to the physical. This will be the first time both will be present on Earth.

6. Golden City Portals. The Golden City is made of a finer substance and has a dimensional weight which anchors it. The apex serves as a portal.

7. The Light of God Never Fails. Simplicity and truth can still cause fear in some due to this different way of thinking. Remember you are a being of peace and harmony, seeking the truth and light of the God that never fails.

8. Weather Crystal. Weather and the Elementals are connected to time. When these are in balance, it is possible to experience timelessness. This gives the harmony to seek within and raise the consciousness to the Ascended level. America holds the focus of light for the world.

9. Spiritual Structure. I AM: Intuition, Armor, Myself. Intuition is used for all that is good and protects. I AM takes us to the heart of God in the clearest, quickest and easiest path. The structure of a pyramid is an example of density at the bottom, with more simplicity and clarity going up, to balance at the apex, where the Ascended Masters are.

10. Universal Energy. Doing and helping are energies of motion, producing an electrical charge that raises the vibration for all. The universal is the motion of spiritual energy.

11. Silence is Golden. But the gold is for the people. I AM is now brought in its total form. Eliminate the fear of being open and let information flow freely. If there is any doubt about someone, ask the I AM Presence to reveal their inner nature before sharing.

12. Ancient Golden Times. Golden Ages are to assist all upcoming and incoming souls. It is an opportunity for all. Those ready to transcend to other levels raise themselves and are lifted.

13. The Descent. There are those who densify into a physical embodiment for spiritual reasons. Within the circle of life is a spiral of different levels of understanding.

14. The Animal Kingdom. The changes in climate will reduce the animal populations and create a need to examine the misconception of requiring a high level of protein in our diets.

15. Food Storage. The crystalline gem structure within chlorophyll is the essence of health and can also be used as an empowering visualization. Networking will assist the maintaining of food sources in Times of Change.

16. Sound. Sound is the Vibration of the Universe. One can travel on the pure notes of God, which are universal and timeless. Sound and light travel out of the physical to other realms. Listen to the sounds woven through the elements.

17. Everlasting Wholeness. Feel yourself as a gold star. Initiations are secret truths shared at inner levels. As the awareness increases of the Ascended Masters, one is surrounded by a circle of light. Earth is a total living organism, whole unto herself, and is often symbolized by the turtle—representing everlasting wholeness. Cosmic Law will manifest what is needed if the desire is not foolish, harmful to another, or harmful to the self. Transform your weakness into your highest shining quality. Use the Violet Flame daily to cleanse, invigorate, and assist with efforts.

Oneness with Earth

18. Travels with the Master. For any trying situation, visualize the Maltese Cross over the heart and call for the higher good. This will be transformational. The energies of gems can be used, the diamond for clarity, the amethyst for transformation and union with the Higher Self, and the emerald for abundance.

19. Portals. Black holes are for interstellar communication. Voids are gateways, assisting and aiding. This cone shape has a self-contained spiraling energy, which slows down as it moves away from the core. The spinning of spiritual energy, interacting with the elements, creates the outer shell of Earth. The core of a cone can be used for communication, opened with love and appreciation. The sun and Earth both contain the female aspect of nurturing and the male aspect of protection. Changes affect all.

20. Three Coins. Within a spiral is the core spiral which holds the passage of the portal. The spinal cord is within a core spiral, the head located at the top. We can learn to speak and manifest through this cord. Like a clear quartz crystal, we also want to be pure and reflect the white light.

21. Communication. Three beams of light emanating from the hand can form an upright triangle which can be used as visualization for tapping into a communication line for all. Quality is in small things and becoming like a child again. A child's motives contain trust. This can set us free.

22. Earth-Shift. A shift happens in the Earth's core first. There is a brilliant white light in the center of Earth, which happened some time ago, and is now moving toward the outer shell. This is a natural process, which happened twice before, paralleling spiritual growth and the Ascension Process. The same is true with us, our inner light is moving outward.

23. Twelve Brothers. Twelve spiritual Brothers unite to send spiritual energy to Earth and humanity at this time for intense spiritual growth and rapid evolution. This is also occurring on many other planets. Solar Awareness is the ability to feel how the sun is an integral part of many other solar systems and its relationship to our Earth. Assist the opening of the inner eye by visualizing yourself sitting on a white cube with pink light all around and within and with gold emanating out from the feet.

24. Map Refinement. You can ask to see the light of the one coming through to assure the highest quality of information. There is a magnetic pull in the center of the Earth's Heart Chakra as it is coming into alignment. The Earth's Heart Chakra is located close to the center of the United States and goes through to the other side of the world in Asia.

25. Completion. The completion of the map holds the end of a cycle and the beginning of the next. The continuing process of change expands consciousness, and this expanding sensation can be uncomfortable at times. *The Book of Truths* is brought through the Blue Ray and the all-seeing Eye of God, stating that the unseen is clearly seen, to live only in the moment, to walk in union, to listen with a kind heart, to be thankful for obstacles, and to learn from others.

26. Judgment. The flaming cross symbolizes everlasting light and union. This is contrasted with a heavy ball, and moving between these two is judgment. With the acceptance of the weight of the world and the acceptance of the light, one can simply choose where to be and let go of the struggle. All paths have had a purpose and have brought us to the wisdom we need in the moment.

27. Seeds of the Future. Remember during this Time of Transition, the seeds that get thrown away with the core will bear fruit again and again. A discovery will be made of a type of tree which grows and produces quickly, utilizing only a carbon-hybrid mist.

28. Kamiak Butte. There are sacred sites with deep, spiritual traditions, such as this mountain of light and Ascension. This is a good place for grounding, feeling the energies of the Mother, and aligning the chakras and light bodies into Oneness.

29. Light Travel. The sweetness of success is the sweetness of knowing yourself. Planets are all ONE, connected through a Web of sound, and can be accessed by adjusting one's energy and projecting. Focus on the navel to ground yourself, the top of the head for the light of protection, and then the Third-Eye Chakra for projecting one's true essence in a triangular shape. Mastery is letting go and surrendering. It is beyond trying, beyond doing and knowing . . . just being.

30. Light and Sound. Light and sound take on a different resonance to produce a different quality of life and are present in all things, also on the Ascended level. As we develop higher awareness, our senses expand. Intersecting vibratory rates, spinning and blending together, determine density. Earth, with two poles, is a replica of the Divine Structure within the Universe. Rotating creates magnetism, enabling growth into a physical form, by gathering and gathering. Feel Oneness by sensing through your own resonance and understand the sameness within all things. Then, you can command. There is always the light.

31. The Storehouse. Future inventions include a ball shape which gives a total physiological adjustment of the Chakra System. It utilizes a magnetic force field to bond energies into a synthesis. Also, there is a triangular shape one can stand in, to intermingle the finer body with the Elemental Life Force for the cleansing of the spiritual.

32. Brotherhood. The Masters extend their hands in service to us as equals, in a continuous, everlasting process. The Pink Ray of unconditional love is most needed for this Transition. Love knows the truth of the Blue Ray and truthful love is the cleansing and transformation of the Violet Ray, taking us from the cocoon to the butterfly. By allowing each person their own truth, we become free. The Christ, the universal principle of love, when seen in all, lifts us into Oneness.

33. Simplicity. Stand back away from judgment. Some lifetimes are fragments, lived to develop a single expression, so that another lifetime can fully bloom. Fragments also need to be nurtured. The acceptance of the Earth Changes is the key to harmony.

34. Time Equals Love. For purifying Earth, call upon the Gold Flame. The cosmic force from the center of the Earth is released. Many taken in the earthquakes will work as guides for others in physical embodiment. A complete cleansing of the Heart Chakra of mankind is needed. This can be accomplished by calling daily, for yourself and for others, upon the protection of Archangel Michael to erase fear to the knowingness of love, with its truth and application. Call upon the Violet Fire and say I AM THAT I AM.

Unity Consciousness

35. Pillars of Service. Turning the will over to the Christ within brings the intuitive knowledge back to Selfhood. Know your place within the universal stream, and you can take command. The Truth of the Ages has no other gods, does not judge, nor covet (infringe upon the freedom of another), and loves one another. These Four Pillars will raise the physical to the level of Ascension. There are no mysteries.

36. Feast of Light. A golden door has opened from the essence and radiance of the Brotherhood, to open minds and hearts for the cleansing and purification of the Mother Planet. The work has gone full circle and returned to the Source, so now it has been refined to its highest message and truth. The unity of force prepares all bodies for Ascension. The true feast is the light of our being. True wisdom recognizes the Source at all times, the Presence which holds all together.

37. Crystalline Structure. The crystalline structure goes through the Veil (which we ourselves have put on) before us. Layer upon layer of points focus energy within. Those which are programmable must be willing to accept new information. The clear quartz is the most receptive. We can access information through the Third Eye Chakra by touching the points or receiving directly with our finer body. We are drawn to crystals to call for their purification and to release our past misuse of this Elemental Life Force. Visualizing the Violet and Green Rays through the Third Eye will assist with its opening. Spiraling these Rays outward assists with purification. As we become clear, open channels, we can access any information desired directly from the Source.

38. Chamber of the Heart. The cleansing and alignment of the Heart Chakra and emotional body is needed for this time of acceleration. Stand with hands outstretched. Flow light into the left hand, circling around the heart, and out the right hand, four times. Through the Third-Eye Chakra, visualize renewed light flowing through it directly to the Heart Chakra, enveloping and cradling it in light. Now, through the Crown Chakra, see sparks of violet light, coming through like stars, surrounding and enveloping the body in a dazzling shower, cleansing your system.

39. Body of Light. We attract dis-ease through slips into a lower vibration. For the healing of the body, focus upon the Green Ray. Visualize this light streaming from the bottom of the feet through to the top of the head, at least twelve times; each time visualize it charging all of your systems, pulsating through you like the circulatory systems.

I AM HEALTHY AT ALL TIMES.
I AM ONE WITH MYSELF AT ALL TIMES.
I AM AT PEACE.

I ask for only that of the purest light to run throughout my system. I ask at all times for the removal of anything which causes disharmony or discord in the functioning of my system. My body is truly the highest expression of light and I will continue expressing my body as a body of light.

40. Journal of Light. All that ever will be is contained in the words I AM. Celebrate! Rejoice in Its power as the Source of all that is. Use the I AM to produce the finest results for bringing into manifestation all that you need. Bless this Presence and say:

I AM HEALTHY, I AM OPULENT, I AM A WELL BEING,
I AM READY TO RECEIVE THAT WHICH GOD HAS
INTENDED FOR ME TO HAVE THIS DAY, I AM A DIVINE
BEING, ONE CENTERED WITHIN THIS UNIVERSE.

Remember at all times, that you are a child of this universe and your parent will provide for you at all times. If ever you are short of money, say:

I AM COMMANDING THE UNIVERSE TO PROVIDE FOR
ME THIS INSTANT AND TO SHOW ME THE CLEAREST
PATH.

Doors will unfold. You are the Divine Inheritors. Spread the Light.

Take in only the purest food and before eating, charge it with the directed activity of the I AM. Recognize the ONE Source in all that you eat and do. Meditate on the points of the Maltese Cross and draw your resonance into the center of its being, for this is the meditation of transformation. There is a directed force which pulls you to the center.

I AM A BEING OF THE VIOLET FLAME, CLEANSED IN
THE HARMONY OF ALL THAT IS.

A rise in consciousness is a rise in balanced thinking. The shift in the poles is an act of balancing, of fine tuning, bringing Earth in harmony with thoughts of harmony and balance. There are those who fear and those who accept, knowing it is the path and that they are guided. They patiently wait for obstacles to be removed and move forward because it is still the path.

The activities of the Elementals cleanse the mass mental and emotional bodies of mankind. Perception is the key. Perceive each moment as the gift that it truly is, a natural progression of things that truly are. Stand back, detach and see with the inner sight and hear with the inner hearing. The Third Eye brings the clear focus of balance, which is the truth. The right use of will and mind bonds with the synthesis of love. This will shed the ego body and bring the emotional body into balance. Stand back without judgment and know within. Meditating in the sun will restore harmony.

41. Six Pivot Points. The transformation of the soul is the integrated Self, occurring through the alignment of six chakra centers, which correspond to the six layers of the human auric field. This is the same for Earth. Initiation is the pathway of discerning, fine-tuning each lesson to experience the universal principle. I AM THAT I AM is true Initiation, aligning six energy points along the meridian, bringing them into total balance.

There are also pivot points which are geographic in nature, which will assist with the early schooling of children, so that they will be able to move with ease with the new energies. These pivot points can also be used for the healing of prejudice and insanity. The criminal mind is a misaligned mind, capable of responding to Divine Intervention. This will bring about the unity with the soul for a planet of peace.

Inner harmony is a continuous meditation upon the soul, which is the seed and the Source. Draw your energies into this ONE Source. Feel it as it anchors within your heart. Then anchor your energies in the pineal gland, located in the center of the brain, up through the top of the head. Five minutes in this state will harmonize the inner, finer bodies and the outer bodies, which correspond to the electro-magnetic field. Earth has a similar core and inner layers, each corresponding to Elemental Life Force, and outer atmospheric layers.

The transformation of the soul is based upon compassion, sharing, giving, and loving. Giving without receiving is the path with the most assured success. Remember what you see in others, you too have felt. We are a bridge to you and you are a bridge to others. So hold out your hands.

42. Center of Inner Sight. The seventh layer of the outer (light) body is the integrated layer, which draws from the six outer bodies. This is where a conical shape begins to form a field, drawing the Higher Self closer to integration. You take in the energies around you and can harmonize them into your seventh layer by gathering up the energies from the inner core of yourself and harmonizing to the outer. This is a cleansing process. This is an activity of love not only for the planet but love of the self.

43. The New Times. If there is a time without a cohesive government, a police state may come about that is formed by the people. Lightworkers can help to organize them in such a way to not harm one another. Much education needs to be disbursed to strong-willed people. The power to raise and distribute food must remain with the people. Fearing, people may forget their God Source. Be prepared to serve from the highest principles.

44. Duality. The solar systems and galaxies also have an interdimensional or etheric structure. Each planet has a Divine Compliment, just as individuals have a splitting off of consciousness, which can also be called a Twin Flame or a Soul Cluster. This mirroring is a common occurrence, like the opposing petals of a flower, and can be misconstrued as another dimension. Our sun is one of twelve within the same Galactic Deity. And we actually have twelve planets. Moving to Fourth Dimension, we can experience the ability to travel to other planets through our consciousness and command physical elements. All life originates from the spiritual realm of consciousness and densifies to the physical level; universal principles apply wherever you go.

Some reports of aliens are actually beings moving from Second to Third Dimension, who do not yet understand the laws of noninterference. Understanding the God Source is an evolutionary step. For noninterference, call upon the Blue Flame of Protection and to Archangel Michael for assistance. While you may wonder about these things, keep your light and focus upon your work in this conscious realm. As things are presented and situations come into your life path, remember we are here to assist and help you.

45. Harmony. The key to the soul is harmony and peace. This comes from blending and working with others. Like a stringed instrument, the strings need to work together. The meaning of a composition comes from the constructive cooperation among many and from this comes harmony and a sense of peace. The challenge in the physical embodiment is to be responsible for the energy you dispense and then attract back to yourself. Like swirling water in a cup, there is a time to be calm.

When calm, you can look deeply to find your light. Love is the continual power which plays the hearts of men, for it is truly the root of the will. At night, in the dream state, we go for higher instruction. It is our choice to remember or not. Do not be frustrated by previous choices, even if a choice was subconscious. It is for the highest good.

46. Agreement. The accountability of actions comes because you can only attract to yourself that which you have previously acted upon. Some things happen which need to be spun away from the source of the soul. This helps us to learn the responsibility of our own energy. The true human experience is the perception of good and evil, also with its eternal love. Call to the Beloved I AM Presence for the eternal protection of the Blue-White Flame. As we move to the higher Fourth Dimension, we will experience only the eternal truths. These are the Law of Love, the Law of Mercy and Forgiveness, and the Activity of Cosmic Principles. The third contains the other two and forms the contract and agreement which is observed throughout the universe.

Love is an energy from which all is comprised. The opposite is fear and doubt. Love is the ability to trust. The Violet Flame is the practicum for understanding the eternal energy of love. The bonding with this energy teaches Divine Acceptance of the self for what it is. To experience Mercy, Forgiveness, Compassion, and Grace, first, you extend these qualities to others. Your ability to transcend all problems is extended to others. Synergy is the combined energy and effort of the mass, which will evolve Earth from the Green to the Violet Ray. Extend this Flame to her.

All of our actions come with the original agreement and commitment we have previously made. When you dream at night and we bring the visions to you, they are only brought to you through your agreement. Remember that those within your life are truly messengers, for our energies are subtle and work with all. This is like the attributes of a parent, assisting you to learn responsibility. Like a bird pushed from the nest, you come back the next spring to nest, just like the parent. Nature teaches you the supreme examples of universal principle. You are truly never separated from the Source and are feeling your wings after you're pushed from the nest. We are all truly ONE.

47. The Safe Harbor. The previous embodiments of the Ascended Masters create a pattern of safety to access. Follow your heart at all times and keep love flowing. This is the synthesis or end result of cooperation. See us as a safe harbor, as our time in the physical was spent with purpose. Following your heart will release you to universal Oneness.

48. Ley lines. We are unaware of many forms of communication. There are those sent out to the universe, to the planet and to the subtle level of the (Galactic) Web. There will be a future device which will tap into this Web, producing an energy field through which one may speak clearly and be heard clearly. This device can also be used to find ley lines that are intersecting points on the grid, having three layers which create a portal. We can learn to travel along these and learn how energy is recycled through these portals. Another reminder about the Violet Flame: it is not only for the healing of the physical body, but is also for the healing of the finer layers (light-bodies) and opens the Third Eye.

49. Time Projection. Use Time Travel for constructive purposes. There is a great responsibility when traveling objectively into the past, and there is no interference allowed whatsoever. When traveling subjectively into the future, there can be personal interaction. When traveling to the past, you go primarily to observe and gather energies. To the future, you go to submit and to be part of. In dreams, this is allowed for specific reasons to use in the present, as an awakening tool. Synthesizing these events enables responsible choices in the present. A group may also travel for lessons from the past or in the future. We will find that the past, present and future are integrated and a Divine Thread runs through it all, giving a sense of timelessness.

For hands-on healing with Sananda (Jesus), first cleanse the Heart Chakra, then call upon the I AM Presence:

> BELOVED I AM PRESENCE, I CALL TO YOU THIS
> MOMENT FOR THE SHARED CONSCIOUSNESS OF THE
> ASCENDED MASTER SANANDA.
> I CALL TO HIS RADIANCE AND BRILLIANCE TO BE
> SHARED WITH THE RADIANCE AND BRILLANCE OF MY
> I AM PRESENCE.

Visualize how to become ONE, merging first at the level of the I AM, the Higher Self, in an embrace. Then, put your hands over your hearts and direct the energy down through the top of your head. The energies pulsate from the Crown Chakra down past the Third Eye and the Throat Chakra to the loving Heart Chakra, forming a great ball of fire. See this great flame in the heart expand, charging through your arms, its resonance felt in the palm of the hands. As in all things, practice makes perfect.

Time may appear to be speeding up, but in fact, light is speeding up. This actually gives more time to be present oriented and expand one's energies into the Higher Self.

50. Use of Collective Energy. Contemplation is a reflection upon the soul's energy, that which has occurred and that which must be collected into one directive force. In stillness, you can closely examine the nature of all your actions. It is necessary to become still, as energies are directed to many uses and each must be stilled to see where they fit. There are many energies which are truly not compatible with yours and need to be removed. Look at the natural self and understand the purpose of that within your being. There is meditation without visualization, a process of becoming calm, of staying in the center balance. Contemplate issues at a deep, core level. There you can discover motives and know whether or not something serves your purpose.

You can allow thoughts to enter the core of your being and decide whether or not they are consistent with your beliefs. As you turn your will over to your life-force, ask for the purpose of the day. Is it a day for peace? Then, with each event, say "I AM at peace."

When you are interacting with others, you have both the collective mind and the collective self. We heal one another as we speak. Healing is the removal of separation and the acceptance of the interaction of another in your path. Merging accepts the self.

51. The Christ Plane. When experiences become intense, you work to dissolve that which hampers or impedes you from where you want to be. On the course of walking the spiritual path, you have lessons which may prompt you to eliminate energy and vibration from yourself that is not needed. Embedded negative energies work their way to the surface. Welcome this, as you are clearing energies from your system, your bodies and the many layers of the etheric and learning the right use of energy. Recognize what is happening for the higher purpose. Beyond channeling is the merging of consciousness. We cannot infringe, but we can ask you to do our work, the work of the God Source, of which we are all ONE. We are here for your assistance. We are from your true Home and gather you under our wings, treating you as one of the flock that you are.

Index

W

waterless bath, the
  new technology 110
weather crystal 35, 81, 225
  definition 223
White Water 19, 23
will
  definition 223
Will of God 123
  and consistent truth 126
wisdom
  "True wisdom is never lost." 152
Wisdom Ray
  and El Morya 152
  definition 223

Z

zero-point 37
  definition 223

About Lori Toye

Lori Toye is not a prophet of doom and gloom. The fact that she became a prophet at all is highly unlikely. Reared in a small Idaho farming community as a member of the conservative Missouri Synod Lutheran church, Lori had never heard of meditation, spiritual development, reincarnation, channeling or clairvoyant sight.

Her unusual spiritual journey began in Washington State, when, as advertising manager of a weekly newspaper, she answered a request to pick up an ad for a local health food store. Upon entering, a woman at the counter pointed a finger at her and said, "You have work to do for Master Saint Germain!"

The next several years were filled with spiritual enlightenment that introduced Lori, then only twenty-two years old, to the most exceptional and inspirational information she had ever encountered. Lori became a student of Ascended Master teachings.

Awakened one night by the luminous figure of Saint Germain at the foot of her bed, her work had begun. Later in the same year, an image of a map appeared in her dream. Four teachers clad in white robes were present, pointing out Earth Changes that would shape the future United States.

Five years later, faced with the stress of a painful divorce and rebuilding her life as a single mother, Lori attended spiritual meditation classes. While there, she shared her experience and encouraged by friends, she began to explore the dream through daily meditation. The four Beings appeared again and expressed a willingness to share the information. Over a six-month period, they gave over eighty sessions of material, including detailed information that would later become the I AM America Map.

Clearly Lori had to produce the map. The only means to finance it was to sell her house. She put her home up for sale, and in a depressed market, it sold the first day at full asking price.

She produced the map in 1989, rolled them on her kitchen table, and sold them through word-of-mouth. She then launched a lecture tour of the northwest and California. Hers was the first Earth Changes Map published, and many others have followed, but the rest is history.

From the tabloids to the *New York Times*, *The Washington Post*, television interviews in the U.S., London, and Europe, Lori's Mission was to honor the material she had received. The material is not hers, she stresses. It belongs to the Masters, and their loving, healing approach is disseminated through the I AM America Publishing Company operated by her husband and spiritual partner, Lenard Toye. Working together, they organized free classes of the teachings and their instructional pursuits led them to form the School of the Four Pillars which included holistic and energy healing techniques. In 1995 and 1996 they sponsored the first Prophecy Conferences in Philadelphia and Phoenix, Arizona.

Other publications include three additional prophecy maps, eight books, a video, and more than sixty audiotapes based on sessions with Master Teacher Saint Germain and other Ascended Masters.

Spiritual in nature, I AM America is not a church, religion, sect, or cult. There is no interest or intent in amassing followers or engaging in any activity other than what Lori and Lenard can do on their own to publicize the materials they have been entrusted with.

They have also been directed to build the first Golden City community. A very positive aspect of the vision is that all the maps include areas called "Golden Cities." These places hold a high spiritual energy, and are where sustainable communities are to be built using solar energy alongside classical feng shui engineering and infrastructure. The first community, Wenima Village, is currently being planned for development.

Concerned that some might misinterpret the Maps' messages as doom and gloom and miss the metaphor for personal change, or not consider the spiritual teachings attached to the maps, Lori emphasizes the Masters stressed that this was a prophecy of choice. Prophecy allows people choice in making informed decisions and promotes the opportunity for cooperation and harmony. Lenard and Lori's vision for I AM America is to share the Ascended Masters' prophecies as spiritual warnings to heal and renew our lives.

Books and Maps by Lori Toye

Books:

NEW WORLD ATLAS SERIES
  Volume One: I AM America
  Volume Two: The Greening Map
  Volume Three: The Map of Exchanges

FREEDOM STAR: *Prophecies that Heal Earth*

GOLDEN CITY SERIES
  Book One: Points of Perception
  Book Two: Light of Awakening
  Book Three: Divine Destiny
  Book Four: Sacred Energies of the Golden Cities

I AM AMERICA TRILOGY
  Book One: A Teacher Appears
  Book Two: Sisters of the Flame
  Book Three: Fields of Light

Maps:

I AM America Map
Freedom Star World Map
United States 6-Map Scenario
United States Golden City Map

I AM AMERICA PUBLISHING & DISTRIBUTING
P.O. Box 2511, Payson, Arizona, 85547, USA. (480) 744-6188

For More Information: **www.loritoye.com**

I AM America Online Bookstore:
http://iamamericabookstore.iaabooks.com

About I AM America

I AM America is an educational and publishing foundation dedicated to disseminating the Ascended Masters' message of Earth Changes Prophecy and Spiritual Teachings for self-development. Our office is run by the husband and wife team of Lenard and Lori Toye who hand-roll maps, package, and mail information and products with a small staff. Our first publication was the I AM America Map, which was published in September 1989. Since then we have published three more prophecy maps, eight books, and numerous audios/CDs based on the channeled sessions with the Spiritual Teachers.

We are not a church, a religion, a sect, or cult, and are not interested in amassing followers or members. Nor do we have any affiliation with a church, religion, political group, or government of any kind. We are not a college or university, research facility, or a mystery school. El Morya told us that the best way to see ourselves is as "Cosmic Beings, having a human experience."

In 1994, we asked Saint Germain, "How do you see our work at I AM America?" and he answered, "I AM America is to be a clearinghouse for the new humanity." Grabbing a dictionary, we quickly learned that the term "clearinghouse" refers to "an organization or unit within an organization that functions as a central agency for collecting, organizing, storing and disseminating documents, usually within a specific academic discipline or field." So inarguably, we are this too. But in uncomplicated terms, we publish and share spiritually transformational information because at I AM America there is no doubt that "A Change of Heart can Change the World."

With Violet Flame Blessings,
Lori & Lenard Toye

For more information or visit our online bookstore, go to:
www.iamamerica.com

To receive a catalog by mail, please write to:
I AM America
P.O. Box 2511
Payson, AZ 85547

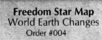

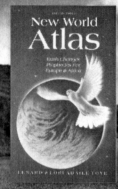

CPSIA information can be obtained at www.ICGtesting.com
Printed in the USA
BVOW021632040613

322238BV00005B/11/P